Travel Health

by **Dr Ted Lankester**

39

37

77

CONTENTS

94

132
85

INTRODUCTION

WHAT ARE THE RISKS?

Travelling anywhere – at home or abroad – involves a certain level of risk to our health and safety. Particularly before long trips, many of us worry that our health may let us down. And we wonder what sort of health care will be available at our destination. Maybe you're the laid-back type who'll only think about mosquito nets 24 hours before going through passport control, and will phone the doctor five days before take-off to ask what jabs are needed. A few sensible measures will help to prevent diarrhoea, dengue, malaria and other hazards. So get informed, take precautions and save yourself trouble. But having had your jabs, collected the right kit and decided to give your health priority, stop worrying about what might (but probably won't) happen.

Let's look at the health problems that are most likely. It's helpful to think of potential problems in two groups: those that are just a nuisance and those that are really serious.

Minor Problems

It isn't hard to guess the main nuisance: traveller's diarrhoea, which goes by many different names just because it's so common. It affects about half of all those travelling from a developed country for a two- to three-week holiday in a developing country. You can do quite a bit to prevent traveller's diarrhoea and a lot to treat it quickly *(see pages 51–60)*.

The other main nuisances are the same sorts of thing we might get back home: coughs, colds, sore throats, a migraine, a flare-up of an existing back problem. Of course, certain destinations, especially in the tropics, have their own hassles: heat rash, bites that sometimes get infected, and just sheer tiredness, especially if the heat, mosquitoes, local dogs and snores from our travelling companions keep us awake.

More Serious Problems

Now, how about the more serious things? Attacks on travellers by snakes, sharks, crocodiles and poisonous creepy crawlies grab the headlines but in reality very rarely pose life-threatening problems. What travellers do need to be careful about are certain diseases which, a few years back, we thought would soon be confined to the history books, thanks to modern medicine. But they've made a comeback; experts call these re-emerging diseases. Other serious risks to travellers include sexually transmitted diseases and road crashes.

Malaria and Other Diseases

The biggest worry is malaria. Three thousand children die from it every day in sub-Saharan Africa alone. Although comparatively few travellers die from this mosquito-borne disease, some do, and many more get seriously ill, nearly always because they didn't take the right precautions. So read pages 61–8 very carefully if you will be visiting any of the areas shown on page 11.

Another serious problem is dengue fever, a flu-like illness that's also spread by a mosquito. In some areas, dengue is more common than malaria. Unlike malaria, dengue can't be prevented, apart from avoiding mosquito bites.

Avian flu has emerged recently as a cause of concern. The dangers to travellers are low but the worry factor is high, which is why this book has a section about the disease *(see pages 115–16)*. Other diseases that often become media scare stories include the plague, ebola and marburg fever. These are extremely rare, and the risk to travellers is just about zero.

Sexually Transmitted Infections
One group of illnesses people should worry about more is sexually transmitted infections. These are extremely common and easy to catch unless travellers opt for abstinence or mutually faithful relationships, or always use a condom. This

Dancing in Mumbai

group of diseases includes HIV and Hepatitis B, both worth avoiding at all costs *(see pages 75–8)*.

Road Crashes

Travellers are most at risk of death or serious injury not from disease or poisonous creatures, but from road crashes. Problems also arise when an accident occurs and health insurance proves to be

Universal sign

inadequate. Nearly 90 percent of crashes are avoidable. Simple precautions, such as not drinking alcohol and driving, not taking drugs, wearing seat belts and avoiding driving at night, greatly reduce the risk. There's more on what travellers can do to minimise the possibility of road crashes on pages 71–3.

AND IF I DO GET ILL?

Even if you take all the recommended precautions, you'll sometimes become ill on your travels. Although the quality of health care varies greatly from country to country, you'll find that most large cities, even in the poorest countries, offer good-quality care if you're prepared to look for it. The same cannot be said for many remote areas *(see page 49)*.

In case you need medical help abroad, it's vital to take out comprehensive travel health insurance, carry documents of any previous illnesses you have had or medication you are taking, and check out the best facilities in any area you will be staying or travelling in for any length of time. Read more about travel insurance on pages 39–41.

ILLNESSES BY REGION

Most illnesses caught by travellers are common conditions that have little to do with the area they are travelling in. The list below is not complete, and many illnesses mentioned are rarely caught by travellers. Travel health advice should be sought which is specific to the country, length of stay and type of activity, all of which are essential to know in assessing risk. Sexually transmitted infections are of course high-risk in all areas.

Caribbean
Greatest risks. Dengue fever, diarrhoea and dysentery.
Lesser risks. Amoebiasis, giardiasis, hepatitis A and B, malaria (in a few islands).

Latin America
Greatest risks. Amoebiasis, dengue fever, diarrhoea and dysentery, giardiasis, hepatitis A and B, malaria (in the tropical jungle), typhoid.
Lesser risks. Bilharzia (NE South America only), Chagas disease (South American sleeping sickness), jigger fleas, leishmanisis, rabies, tuberculosis, yellow fever.

South Asia
Greatest risks. Amoebiasis, dengue fever, diarrhoea and dysentery, giardiasis, hepatitis A and B, malaria, rabies, typhoid.
Lesser risks. Chikungunya fever, cholera, filariasis, Japanese encephalitis.

East and Southeast Asia
Greatest risks. Amoebiasis, dengue fever, diarrhoea and dysentery, giardiasis, hepatitis A and B, malaria, rabies, typhoid.
Lesser risks. Bilharzia (schistosomiasis) in a few areas only, cholera, filariasis, Japanese encephalitis, typhus.

Sub-saharan Africa

Greatest risks. Amoebiasis, bilharzia (shistosomiasis), diarrhoea and dysentery, giardiasis, hepatitis A and B, jigger fleas, malaria, meningitis (meningococcal), rabies, tick-bite fever, Tumbu fly bites, typhoid.

Lesser risks. Brucellosis, cholera, dengue fever, filariasis, Lassa fever (West Africa), Rift Valley fever, river blindness, sleeping sickness, yellow fever.

Middle East and North Africa

Greatest risks. Diarrhoea and dysentery, giardiasis, typhoid.

Lesser risks. Amoebiasis, brucellosis, hepatitis A and B, leishmaniasis, rabies.

Europe and Central Asia

Greatest risks. Giardiasis, Lyme disease, tick-borne encephalitis.

Lesser risks. Amoebiasis, typhoid.

Oceania

Greatest risks. Dengue fever, diarrhoea and dysentery, malaria (some only).

Lesser risks. Amoebiasis, filariasis, giardiasis, hepatitis A and B, typhoid, typhus.

North America

Lesser risks. Lyme disease, Rocky Mountain spotted fever, West Nile virus.

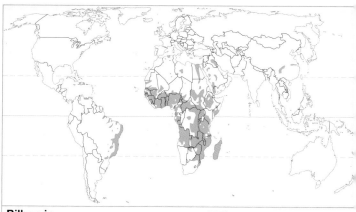

Bilharzia

The exact distribution of *Bilharzia* is subject to change

Areas where bilharzia is found

Based on WHO data

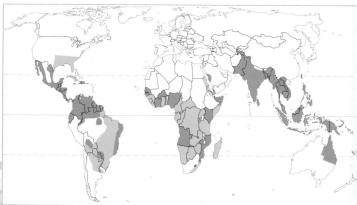

Dengue Fever

The exact distribution of *Dengue Fever* is subject to change

Areas with *Aedes aegpyti* and
recent dengue epidemic activity

Areas infested with *Aedes aegypti*

Based on CDC Travelers' Health data

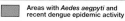

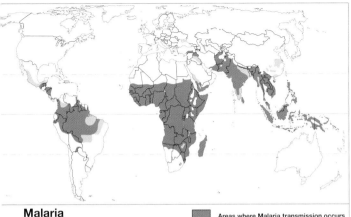

Malaria

The exact distribution of *Malaria* is subject to change

Areas where Malaria transmission occurs

Areas with limited risk

Based on WHO data

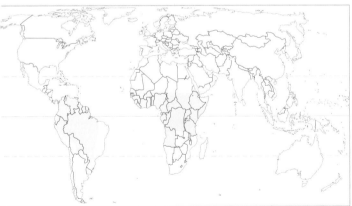

Yellow Fever

Countries/areas where there is a risk of Yellow Fever Transmission

Based on WHO data

BEFORE YOU TRAVEL

A TRAVEL HEALTH CHECKLIST

There's a lot to do before travelling abroad – booking airline tickets, checking your passport's up to date, getting the necessary visas. Just as important is ensuring your health and safety. The advice below is intended to help make your trip a trouble-free one.

Vaccinations

They may be inconvenient, expensive and occasionally painful, but vaccinations cut down the number of serious things that might happen to you, and having them will keep your travel health insurance company happy. Think about getting vaccinations three months before you go. If you need a yellow fever jab, make sure you obtain a signed and stamped certificate, otherwise Mr Difficult at border X might give you trouble.

Antimalarials

If malaria may be present at your destination, get advice about whether you need to take pills to prevent this disease, and if so what to take, when to start and how to remember to take them. Although no medication is 100 percent effective or completely free of side effects, it's important to remember that by taking regular malaria prevention tablets (antimalarials) you will reduce your chance of being medically evacuated or spending time in the local hospital. And your holiday, project or expedition is less likely to be ruined. Remember: malaria can be fatal.

Repellents and Mosquito Nets

Repellents and nets reduce your chances of getting malaria. They also keep those whining mosquitoes at bay (not to mention other interesting creatures wanting to check you out during the night), and nets help falling spiders bounce onto the floor while you sleep on blissfully unaware. Nets should be impregnated with an insecticide such as permethrin. The most effective personal insect repellents contain Deet *(see page 62)*.

First-Aid or Health Kit

It's worth taking a first-aid or health kit if you are going to a developing country or will be travelling off the beaten path anywhere in the world. Some travellers may baulk at the expense, but a kit is handy to have when you don't trust the local needles, your boils burst or the Swiss Army knife slips and your hand starts to spurt blood. There's more on these and other health supplies on pages 32–4.

Travel Insurance

It's essential to have a travel insurance policy with medical cover. Check that it covers the places you're travelling to and the kinds of activities you'll be doing. If you'll be doing adventure sports, make sure these are covered. If you have any pre-existing medical conditions, such as asthma or diabetes, or you're pregnant, make sure your policy covers anything that may happen as a direct result. There's a huge choice in the insurance world, so get two or three quotes. See pages 39–41 for more details.

If you're a UK citizen and your destination is in Europe, obtain a European Health Insurance Card by post or online. This card helps you to obtain free emergency health care in many European countries: it's easiest to do an internet search to find the details.

Personal Medicines

Have with you enough of any medication you usually use, plus a prescription or letter. Take enough of the pills and potions you needed on your last trip, or that you predict you might need if your recurring itch, pain, headache or allergy pops up in Bangkok or Burkina Faso. Remember the other things you may need, too: the contraceptive pill perhaps, contact lens solutions, tampons, suncream. Then think about taking a medical kit if you're doing a long or adventurous trip to the wild beyond. In case of loss or theft, divide any supplies you take between 'hand and hold' (cabin and aircraft-hold luggage), apart from insulin, which may be destroyed by the freezing conditions of the aircraft hold.

Camping in the wilds of Alaska

Doctors and Dentists

If you've got any health worries, see a doctor before you travel – either your usual doctor or a travel health specialist. And unless you have five-star teeth, have a dental check-up at least two weeks before you go. Don't risk a raging toothache in a dentist-free zone.

Know Your Blood Group

For adventure travel, a gap year or a longer stint abroad, it's a good idea to know your blood group. The value of knowing it is in case of needing an urgent transfusion in a remote area, so you can ascertain whether any colleagues with you may have the same or a compatible group (although blood always has to be 'cross-matched' with any donor's blood before you receive it). Record your blood group on your passport, immunisation record, or in a wallet. In the UK and some other countries a good way to discover your blood group is to become a blood donor.

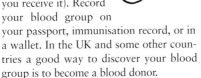

Going to a Developing Country?

If you are going to a developing country, arrange a travel health consultation with your doctor, practice nurse or a travel medicine specialist. If you have difficulty finding someone who is well informed about your destination, look at some of the websites on page 142.

PRE-EXISTING HEALTH PROBLEMS

Many people have a health problem that may affect their trip. If you have ever been seriously ill, had a recent operation or injury, have any medical problem that affects your daily living or are taking any medication, then talk to your doctor. The point of doing this is, first, to make sure it's safe to travel, but just as important, to know if you should take any special precautions. Here are some conditions that are common or important. Of course, it's not a complete list.

Allergic Reactions

If you have ever had an anaphylactic reaction (severe itchy swellings, swollen lips or tongue and difficulty breathing) to, for example, peanuts, treenuts, wasps, bees, other flying creatures or edible substances, then do the following. Take two self-injection adrenalin (epinephrine) kits, commonly known as Epipens. Have one on you all the time. In many countries you will need a prescription to obtain an Epipen, and if you are going from one country to another you should also have

What to Do Before You Go

– See your GP or specialist to discuss your trip.
– Work out a plan if your health problem worsens.
– Take adequate medical supplies, including standby antibiotics if relevant.
– Put supplies in different parts of your luggage in case of loss or theft.
– If you have a serious illness or allergy obtain and wear a Medicalert bracelet or pendant <www.medicalert.org.uk>.
– Make sure any medication you take does not interact with any anti-malarial or other travel medication you may need.
– At your destination, make sure you know where the best hospital or doctor is, just in case you run into a problem.

a signed letter from your doctor saying this is for your personal medical use only. If you need to use one when travelling you must see a doctor as soon as possible, as it's common to get a further allergic reaction after you have apparently recovered.

If you just develop severe swelling at the site of any bite, but no generalised rash, or hives, urticaria or a breathing problem, or swollen mouth or tongue, just take care and take chlorphenamine (Piriton) 4mg, one or two as soon as you can (it may make you drowsy).

Polluted cities can aggravate asthma

Asthma

In some countries of the northern hemisphere, up to 25 percent of people have a wheezy tendency. Travel is only likely to be a problem if your asthma can be severe or unpredictable. Take special care if one or more of the following applies to you: you use inhaled steroids regularly; you need your bronchodilator, such as salbutamol (Ventolin), at least once a day; in the past five years you've had to go to hospital with an asthma attack; or you've had to use a nebuliser or have taken steroid tablets, for example prednisolone.

Usually asthma gets less frequent and less severe

when you get to the tropics, but not always, especially if you are in a smoggy, polluted city such as Cairo, Mexico City, Mumbai or Lima. Sometimes a dry, dusty atmosphere can also make it worse. Get special advice if you plan to go to altitudes above 3,000m (about 10,000ft) or want to go diving *(see pages 86–9)*.

Back Problems

The excitement of travel, carrying backpacks and being in a hurry can often cause or exacerbate back problems. If your back has ever seized up or you have been off work in the past year because of severe backache or sciatica (pain or numbness down the leg), talk to your doctor before travelling.

Bowel Problems

Nearly one-third of the UK population has symptoms of irritable bowel syndrome (IBS). Sometimes travel can make this condition worse, especially if you also pick up traveller's diarrhoea or dysentery. If you have IBS you'll have to learn what foreign foods suit you best – whether high or, sometimes, low in fibre. Consider taking some mebeverine (Colofac) 135mg tablets with you to help the cramps (it has to be prescribed in the UK and some other countries), or anything else you know that eases the pain.

Other Bowel Problems

Those with coeliac disease or Crohn's disease should see their doctor for specific advice. Haemorrhoids can get worse with travel, especially if you get constipated – have any rectal bleeding checked before you leave.

Peptic ulcers and indigestion can get worse when travelling. Because ulcers sometimes bleed, see your doctor before travelling if you get recurring pain in the stomach. Diverticular disease can flare up overseas, sometimes triggered by a bowel infection. Take a standby antibiotic with you, such as ciprofloxacin 500mg, if you have had this problem before, and a tablet to deal with the spasm such as hyoscine (Buscopan) 10mg.

Chronic Fatigue

If you have chronic fatigue syndrome (CFS or ME), it's best not to go travelling for more than a very short trip. The stress and excitement of overseas travel can bring this on or make it worse unless you have fully recovered, having had at least three months feeling largely back to normal. If in doubt, talk it over with your doctor.

If you're someone who tires easily, see your doctor to make sure there's no treatable cause, such as anaemia, and don't try to pack too much into your trip. Taking regular exercise can often help to relieve tiredness.

Depression and Anxiety

Depression and anxiety vary so much that it is hard to make any rules. If you are taking antidepressants, it's usually best to continue these during your trip. Sometimes, but by no means always, the stress of being away from familiar surroundings and from family and friends can make things worse. If you need to take an antimalarial, don't use mefloquine (Lariam). Talk to your doctor if you are taking

The perfect place to unwind

medication or have had time off school, college or work in the past few years because of depression or anxiety.

Diabetes

Unless your diabetes is difficult to control or has come on recently, you should be able to travel, but get detailed advice from your diabetic specialist. This must include how to manage time zones, and if you're on insulin, guidance on adjusting dosage.

Precautions

• Take all supplies with you, keeping these in two different places in case of loss or theft. Keep insulin in your hand luggage as it can freeze in the aircraft hold.

• Discuss your trip in detail with your diabetic adviser.

• Know how to manage your dosage when crossing time zones, or managing severe heat, diarrhoea, dehydration or fever. Try to avoid these where possible.

• Take special care of your skin, and wear comfortable footware.

• Have a system of dealing with hypos, for example always have sweets or dextrose to hand, or carry some Hypostop Gel or glucagon for injection by a companion.

• On arrival at your destination, check out good medical facilities in case of severe problems.

• Take a doctor's letter with you, which must include details of insulin dosage, and a statement that all needles and syringes etc. are for your personal use.

• Make sure you can store insulin in a darkened place at the recommended temperature when abroad: above freezing, but below 25°C (77°F). If your destination is very hot, consider taking a stainless steel vacuum flask for storing insulin.

• Contact Diabetes UK at <www.diabetes.org.uk>, or your own national diabetes organisation.

Epilepsy

If you have epilepsy that is not reliably controlled by medication, it is best not to go abroad. If your condition is well

controlled, you should be OK, but it pays to discuss your trip with your doctor before leaving.

Precautions
• Bring ample supplies of the medicines you take, stored in different parts of your luggage.
• If going to malarious areas, take special precautions, because fever occasionally triggers an attack.
• Don't use mefloquine or chloroquine, either to prevent or treat malaria. Seek advice from a travel medicine specialist.
• Make sure any travelling companions know about your condition.

Glandular Fever

If you've recently suffered from glandular fever (infectious mononucleosis), don't go on any long overseas trips until you are completely better. Unless you had a very mild dose, or your trip is very short, it is worth having two or three months feeling fully recovered before going abroad, otherwise you may have a relapse if you get tired or run-down.

Heart Problems

If you have a heart condition, see your doctor for specific advice. When travelling, take ample supplies of medicine with you, together with a letter summarising your condition and the tablets you are taking, and a copy of your latest ECG. Check that medication you are taking does not interact with travel medication, such as antimalarials.

Angina
If you suffer from angina, travel only if this condition has been investigated and is well controlled. Plan your trip with care and get specific medical advice. If your control is good, you can do reasonable exercise and go to moderate elevations.

Coronary Bypass and Heart Attack

If you've had a coronary bypass operation, travel when the specialist says it is safe to do so and when you feel well and confident. In many instances you will be able to plan a ro-

Pacemakers

People with pacemakers should note that some pacemakers may occasionally trigger airport metal detectors or very rarely malfunction due to airport scans. Check with the manufacturer about airport security systems and take a note of the model with you.

bust travel itinerary with plenty of exercise and go to moderate or sometimes high altitudes, providing you get no adverse symptoms at home and have obtained expert medical advice.

If you've suffered a heart attack, see your doctor for advice. Travel only when you have fully recovered and feel confident.

Raised Blood Pressure

Make sure high blood pressure is well controlled, and keep strictly to your medication. Have your blood pressure measured regularly.

HIV

There is no medical reason not to travel if you are HIV positive, providing you are well and have regular check-ups. If you are going abroad for any length of time, have a CD4 count and, if possible, a viral load check before you go and talk to your specialist. A few countries won't give you a visa. If you intend to work abroad, some occupations are a no-go, such as doing midwifery or any exposure-prone procedures. If you are taking anti-retrovirals, make sure you either take enough with you or can reliably get hold of the ones you need at your destination. Some immunisations may not be recommended, and check there are no interactions between your antiretroviral therapy (ART) and any travel medications. It can be difficult to get travel insurance.

Removed Spleen

If you've had your spleen removed, you're more likely to get infections, including malaria, and to get them more seriously. Most travellers do very well if they take precautions.

> the spleen...er it's here or here

Precautions
• Have all your travel jabs, including meningitis ACWY and pneumococcal vaccine.
• Take malaria very seriously – both preventing it and treating it. Consider travelling in malaria-free zones only.
• Talk to your doctor about taking prophylactic antibiotics or a standby course in case you come down with an infection.

Skin Problems

Eczema can occasionally flare up in hot and humid conditions and become infected. If this has ever happened, talk to your doctor and take a supply of creams with you and standby antibiotics. Eczema often improves in warmer climates.

Fungal infections are more prone to occur in the tropics; athlete's foot, candida (thrush) and ringworm are the commonest. Get these treated if they occur, otherwise they can cause itching and keep you awake at night, and affected areas may become further infected.

Psoriasis often improves in sunny climates. If you suffer from psoriasis, avoid taking chloroquine for malaria prevention or treatment.

Weight Problems

Underweight

Be realistic about this. If you have been anorexic (down to a Body Mass Index of 18 or less, or your periods have stopped because of restricted food intake), get specialist advice about travelling, except for a very short trip. For long trips, say three months or more, it makes sense not to travel for at least a year after your weight has largely got back to normal. Why? Because if you get ill or develop diarrhoea, you can become seriously underweight. Also, stress overseas can sometimes trigger an eating problem, whether anorexia or bulimia.

Overweight

If your problem is at the other end of the scale (your Body Mass Index is 35 or more), it's worth trying to lose weight before you go. Otherwise the heat can feel that bit worse, you can tire more easily and it can be a sweat – a literal sweat – keeping up with travel companions. You also have a greater risk of developing a deep vein thrombosis (DVT) during travel, and skin infections in hot climates can be more of a nuisance.

VACCINATIONS

Here's a list of the travel vaccines you may need to have if you're travelling from a developed to a developing country. See your doctor, nurse or a travel health specialist to work out exactly what you need for your particular trip. Otherwise look at a reliable website (see page 142).

(see page 142)

Recommendations vary between countries and between specialists. The list below is taken from a range of expert opinion. A code such as 0, 7–14, 28 means: have the second jab 7 to 14 days after the first and the third 28 days after the first; a few days either way makes little difference. It's better to delay immunisations if you're unwell, especially if you have a fever, but still make sure you complete the course.

> **Start early**
>
> If you need a lot of vaccinations, especially rabies, hepatitis B or Japanese encephalitis, you ideally need to start three months before you leave. It's a waste of time and money going to Kabale or Kathmandu with your jabs half done (although having some is better than having none). Give your immune system a bit of priority!

BCG for Tuberculosis

Experts are not agreed on this, and some countries don't use BCG at all. It is usually recommended for infants under six months, and for health workers and others likely to be in contact with TB patients. BCG does not need to be repeated if you've previously had one, or have had a positive Tuberculin test (also known as PPD, Mantoux, Tine or Heaf).

Cholera

Cholera is extremely rare in travellers, but there is an effective oral vaccine. You should have it if you're doing front-line work in refugee camps or travelling in poor communities where cholera outbreaks commonly occur. The vaccine also gives partial protection against some common forms of traveller's diarrhoea for up to three months. Get expert advice. Two doses are given between one and six weeks apart.

Diphtheria and Tetanus

If you've had a course of three primary injections as a child, you'll need booster doses every 10 years, so ensure that you're in-date before travelling. If you've never had these before, talk to your doctor about having a course of three injections one month apart if you're doing remote or long-term travel.

Hepatitis A

Get vaccinated for any trip to a developing country. One jab lasts for a year, and a second given 6 to 24 months later gives protection for up to 20 years. See also hepatitis B, below.

A local drug store in the Caribbean

Hepatitis B

You get this disease mainly from dirty needles and unprotected sex. Get vaccinated if you're a health worker, giving hands-on health care, working with children, taking part in high-risk activities (discuss with your doctor), or if you're going for more than a month to a developing country, Eastern Europe or the former Soviet Union. Normal schedule (in months): 0, 1, 2, 6–12, but some clinics can give you an accelerated course that takes only a month with a subsequent booster.

If you were brought up in a developing country, you may have developed natural immunity to hepatitis A or B. This can be checked with a blood test, and if positive means you will not need immunisation. The hepatitis B test may occasionally show you are infectious or have liver damage from a previous, usually unknown, infection with the virus, so discuss this with your doctor before having this test.

Influenza and Pneumococcal

Have vaccinations for these if you're over 65 or have heart or lung disease, diabetes or lowered immunity. Also consider having flu vaccine if going on a cruise ship or taking a long-term trip. Make sure you're given the current recommended flu vaccine for whichever hemisphere you'll be travelling in. Main risk times for flu: winter in the northern hemisphere, April to September in the southern. A recent flu vaccine is now requested for the Hajj pilgrimage.

Japanese Encephalitis (JE)

Get vaccinated if you're going to spend more than a month in rural areas of South and Southeast Asia, at a time of year when the disease is prevalent. Normal schedule: 0, 7–14, 28, with boosters every two to three years for the most commonly used brand. You should ideally not travel until 10 days after completing the course because of occasional delayed side effects.

Meningitis

Consider this if you're going to a country bordering the southern Sahara (Sahel region). Distribution of meningitis varies, so get specialist advice. The ACWY jab is more expensive than the commonly used vaccine against strains A and C, but covers more varieties. It involves one injection every three years. A certificate showing you've had the vaccine in the last three years is needed for the Hajj pilgrimage to Mecca and for the Umrah.

Polio

Polio has not yet been eradicated. Get vaccinated if you're going to a developing country, especially if polio is still occurring there. You'll need to have one single booster if you have completed a primary course of three immunisations as a child.

Rabies

Get vaccinated if you're going to be more than 24 hours from a capital city in Africa, Asia or Latin America, or if you're going for more than a month to a country where rabies is common. There are a number of different types of vaccine used for preventing rabies. It is ideal but not essential that you use the same type for the full course of injections (see page 69).

There's a shortage of the life-saving rabies immunoglobulin that must be given immediately after a risky bite if you haven't had your pre-travel jabs, so rabies immunisation is very important. Schedule: 0, 7, 21–28, with a booster after three years, thereafter every five years. Always seek expert medical advice immediately after any animal bite.

Tick-Borne Encephalitis

Get vaccinated if you're going to the forests of Eastern, Central or Northern Europe, or Central Asia during the summer for one month or more. Get specific advice. Schedule: two doses 4 to 12 weeks apart and ideally a booster 5 to 12 months later.

Typhoid

Get vaccinated for any trip to a developing country, Eastern Europe or the former Soviet Union, unless the trip is short and to high-grade accommodation. The biggest risk is in South Asia. The vaccine can be given as a single jab that lasts for three years or as an oral preparation taken three times on alternate days on an empty stomach.

Yellow Fever

Get vaccinated if you're going to the yellow fever zone of tropical Africa or Latin America *(see map on page 11)*, or have travelled from a country in the yellow fever zone in the last six days to another country that demands a certificate. Yellow fever vaccine is used with caution in those over 60 or with certain medical problems. One jab lasts 10 years: be sure to obtain a signed certificate and carry it with you.

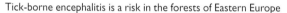

Tick-borne encephalitis is a risk in the forests of Eastern Europe

HEALTH SUPPLIES TO TAKE WITH YOU

Not everyone needs a kit, but it's important to take one if your destination is a developing country or if you intend to travel in remote places anywhere.

Syringe and Needle Kit
Worldwide, 12 million cases of hepatitis B per year are caused by unsterilised, reused needles. Taking clean, sterile needles, to be used in case of emergency, is worth doing for most developing countries. Please note that you will not be able to take these in your hand luggage on a plane.

Diarrhoea Kit
These kits contain oral rehydration sachets or a measuring spoon to make up your own solution, plus a bowel blocker (loperamide) and magic-bullet antibiotic (ciprofloxacin) – extremely handy if either you or your trip are very important, or

that romantic holiday must not have unromantic interruptions. 'Cipro' successfully treats about 70 percent of traveller's diarrhoea. Such kits or equivalent supplies are recommended for all travellers going to developing countries for all but the shortest trips. But when it comes to self-treatment, see a doctor if you have more than five stools in 24 hours or have a fever, or if there's blood in your stool *(see page 56)*.

Medical Kit

A good medical kit contains medicines you might need in remote areas where there's no reliable, well-stocked hospital or clinic with a competent doctor or nurse within reach. Before you go make sure you know what each of the medicines is used for, and when abroad seek medical care if at all possible. If the medicine kit includes prescription-only medicines, you'll usually need to talk to a doctor before they can be supplied. Read patient information leaflets carefully.

First-Aid Kits

A sensible inclusion for most travellers is a first-aid kit. Kits range from simple ones containing plasters and other handy items, to more advanced types containing needles and syringes.

General. Cotton wool, crepe bandage, gauze swabs, mediswabs, zinc oxide or micropore tape, non-adherent dressings, plasters or Band-aids, safety pins, scissors, triangular bandage, tweezers, instructions, letter for Customs, contents list.

Needles and syringes. Usually as 2ml syringes and 23-gauge needles.

Medicines. Basic supplies include: antibiotics, eg amoxicillin or erythromycin, loperamide and ciprofloxacin for diarrhoea, antiseptic cream for infected skin and cuts, hydrocortisone cream for bites and itchy skin conditions, cinnarizine for travel sickness, paracetamol or ibuprofen for pain relief and fever, chlorphenamine for allergies and itching.

Other Useful Items

• Iodine tablets to debug unclean water and neutralising tablets to improve the taste.
• A portable water purifier and water bottle if you're doing lots of remote travel.
• High-factor suncream, a hat, dark glasses or goggles.
• Antibacterial hand-cleaning gel to kill germs without needing water (it should contain at least 60 percent alcohol).
• A thermometer, especially if going to a malarious area or travelling with children.
• Oral contraceptive pill and condoms.

SUPPLIES FOR MALARIOUS AREAS

If you're going to a malarious area, there are some items that you must have. If possible, check first to see if they are available at your destination.
• A permethrin-impregnated mosquito net.
• Insect repellent, preferably Deet-based (20–50 percent Deet).
• Pills to prevent malaria, also known as antimalarials or prophylactics *(see below)*.
• Malaria standby treatment, unless you're travelling for a week or less, or will be entirely based in cities or areas where there are reliable health-care facilities and the recommended good-quality malaria treatment is always available. For recommendations about what type of standby treatment to take, see pages 65–6.

Antimalarials

It can be a real challenge when it comes to deciding which antimalarial to take, as there's more of a choice than a few years ago. Your friends will make suggestions; the internet may leave you in a muddle. To get just the right antimalarial for you and your trip, talk to a travel health adviser – someone who can sit

down with you and take into account just where you'll be going and what you'll be doing, and how long you will be going for.

The main antimalarial drugs are mefloquine, doxycycline, Malarone, chloroquine and proguanil.

Mefloquine

Also known as Lariam, mefloquine is very effective for sub-Saharan Africa and most other areas where there is chloroquine resistance. It is not effective in forested border areas of Thailand, Myanmar, Laos and Cambodia.

How safe? About one person in three gets minor, but sometimes annoying, side effects, including vivid dreams, troubled sleeping and feeling edgy. Major side effects are rare but can be serious and frightening.

What's the dose? One 250mg tablet per week starting three weeks before you go, so you can change to a different antimalarial if your body, mind and mefloquine don't hit it off. Continue for four weeks after leaving a malarious area.

Who shouldn't use it? You shouldn't take it if you have had depression, anxiety, panic attacks or convulsions. It is also best avoided if you're 'moody', don't sleep well, have heart problems, or have used hard or soft drugs. It's now generally considered safe to take in pregnancy and when breastfeeding. **How long can you use it?** Providing you don't have side effects in the short term, the UK Advisory Committee on Malaria Prevention (ACMP) advises that it can be used for at least three years.

Make sure you read the patient information leaflet and speak to a doctor or travel nurse before using mefloquine.

Doxycycline
This antibiotic is familiar to many as a treatment for acne. It is very effective in most parts of the world.
How safe? Unlikely to give serious side effects. However, you may get sunburn more easily, especially if you are fair or freckly. It can cause a sore gullet (oesophagus) unless you swallow it with plenty of fluids and don't lie down just after taking it. It may bring on thrush (candida) or other fungal infections, so women prone to thrush should have fluconazole 150mg available or another suitable preparation.

Ignore Malaria at Your Peril

Recently an experienced aid worker went to work in a remote part of Africa. She was given a detailed briefing and supplied with both antimalarials and standby treatment. However, she decided not to take antimalarials. After eight months she developed a severe attack of malaria, and had to be rushed to a local hospital where she was put on an intravenous drip; for 48 hours her life was in danger. A colleague spent days looking after her and making emergency arrangements. She subsequently had to be repatriated.

The moral of the story is clear. If you don't follow advice on how to avoid malaria, you put your life at risk and inconvenience your companions.

Occasionally it causes a severe headache, in which case you should stop taking doxycycline immediately.

During the first three weeks of taking doxy, those on the contraceptive pill may not be fully protected, and will therefore need to take other precautions. Talk to your doctor about this. The rules are complicated and need to be followed carefully.

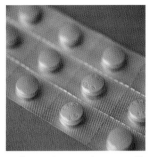

Remember to take your pills

What's the dose? One 100mg capsule daily, starting 24–48 hours before going to a malarious area and continuing for four weeks after leaving.

Who shouldn't use it? Children under 12 (in the US eight is given as the cut-off point), pregnant women, breastfeeding mothers and anyone who has had skin cancer.

How long can you use it? Providing you have no side effects and it's not burning your skin, experts believe it can be used for at least two years.

Malarone

Malarone is a rising star, but it may threaten your bank balance if you're taking a long trip. Malarone consists of proguanil 100mg and atovaquone 250mg. It is very effective against serious, P. falciparum malaria, but slightly less effective for so-called benign malaria. Malarone is also an excellent emergency standby treatment unless you are using it as a prophylactic. The adult dose for treatment is four tablets daily for three days, total 12.

How safe? Few serious side effects have been reported. It occasionally causes an upset stomach and mouth ulcers.

What's the dose? One tablet daily with food, starting 24 hours

High-risk category

You have a high risk of getting malaria if you were
brought up in a malarious
area and are now going
back to visit friends and relatives after living in a non-
malarious area for some
time. Follow the advice below carefully, and also read
the section on pages 61–8.

before going to a malarious
area, but only needing to be
taken for seven days after
leaving, significantly shorter
than other antimalarials.

Who shouldn't use it? Pregnant mothers and those in
the early months of breastfeeding. Also avoid taking
it if you have had bad side
effects when taking pro-
guanil (Paludrine).

How long can you use it? The ACMP advice is that Malarone
can be used for up to one year or longer, but any side effects
should be reported. If you are unable to take mefloquine or
doxycycline and you are going to a malarious area, Malarone
is usually your best prophylactic to cover the trip. Also for
short trips its cost is more reasonable, because you only need
to take it for one week after leaving a malarious area, not
four weeks as with other antimalarials.

Chloroquine and Proguanil

Chloroquine (Nivaquine, Avloclor) and proguanil (Paludrine)
are generally used together, chloroquine (150mg 'base'
tablets) two per week, proguanil (100mg tablets) two per
day. They come in handy combined travel packs. Ideally, start
chloroquine seven days before entering a malarious area,
proguanil 24 hours before, and continue both for four weeks
after leaving. They are safe for pregnant women.

    Unfortunately this combination, which used to work well
in most malarious areas, is becoming less and less effective.
For Africa, Southeast Asia, Assam and the Amazon, the
chloroquine–proguanil combination is no longer an option,
and the list of areas where it no longer works is growing.

TRAVEL INSURANCE

Without insurance, you may be faced with huge expenses and a great deal of hassle if you become ill or are involved in an accident. That's why taking out full and comprehensive travel insurance is so important. Travel insurance is big business, so get two or three quotes from different companies. You will have two aims. The first is to find a policy that covers the places you are going to and the activities you will be doing. The second aim is to get the best value you can.

The insurance companies will be providing two services. The first is insurance as detailed below. The second is access to emergency assistance if the worst happens. By phoning the emergency helpline, the assistance company which works with the insurer will arrange the best treatment available as quickly as possible, including, if necessary, flying you out to the nearest good-quality hospital, or sometimes flying you home.

If you're being insured by the company or agency you're working for, make sure that all the points under Choosing a Policy *(see page 40)* are covered.

Most insurance companies offer single trip or multi-trip

Make sure all adventure sports you plan to do are covered by your travel insurance policy

Accidents can happen

policies. Choose whichever fits in best with your plans. Many
regular travellers just renew their existing policies each year,
but remember it is to your advantage to tell the company of
any new health problems that arise.

Choosing a Policy

Your policy should cover you for all the countries you plan
to visit or find yourself going to, any activities you plan to
do or find yourself doing, and the full length of your stay.
You should be covered for the following:

• Medical, dental and emergency expenses abroad, including medical evacuation (medivac) when needed.
• 24-hour emergency assistance in case of severe illness or
accident.
• Availability of fully screened blood within 24 hours (the
Blood Care Foundation can also arrange this, *see page 142*).

• Personal accident insurance to cover death and disability.
• Personal liability insurance to cover for injury to third parties, including legal costs.
• Cover for emergency care in your home country or any other country where you're treated.
• Cancellation or curtailment of your trip due to your own ill health or that of a close family member or business associate.
• Loss of money and loss, theft or damage to baggage, personal possessions and documents.
• Hijack.
• If you are doing any adventure sports, make sure you are covered for the ones you expect to do. If you are pregnant or might become pregnant, check that any pregnancy-related illness is covered and that any health problem in the newborn will also be covered.

Special Conditions

Some conditions mean that you will have to hunt hard and negotiate for your travel insurance. These include:

• Being an older traveller – but with a higher premium you should find cover.
• Having a significant disability.
• Having an existing medical condition. It's important to declare any existing health problems, or you may find yourself without cover in the event of a claim. Many companies won't cover you for medical conditions arising from a health problem that was present before you travelled. Some may offer cover for a higher premium.
• Being HIV positive.
• Visiting a country that your country advises is unsafe. In the case of UK citizens, the authority which decides these things is the Foreign and Commonwealth Office, <www.fco.gov.uk>.
• If you're working in an insecure area or war zone.

FLYING

DVT

A deep vein thrombosis (DVT) is a blood clot that forms in a vein, usually in the leg. It's dangerous if a small part of the clot breaks off and wanders into the lung.

Your leg veins start objecting on long flights (five hours or longer, but there is no real cut-off point), especially if there is little chance to stretch them, you spend a long time asleep or you are jammed into a window seat. To avoid the risk of a DVT forming, this is what you should do:

• Stretch and flex your leg muscles frequently while in your seat – several times an hour.
• Get up and walk around every hour or so if possible.
• Have plenty to drink (water or soft drinks) and not too much alcohol, tea or coffee.
• Watch the pre-flight video on DVT that many airlines now show routinely while being cleared for take-off, or read the section in the in-flight magazine.

DVT-Prone

Some people are at greater risk of developing a DVT. If you come into any of the following categories, see your doctor for advice.

- pregnant women
- those who have recently had surgery
- those who have a serious or chronic illness
- people with varicose veins
- women taking the contraceptive pill
- women having HRT
- those who are overweight
- those with a personal or family history of DVT

If you have one or more of the risk factors in the box opposite, you'll need to wear firmly fitting below-knee stockings (graded compression stockings). Although there is no evidence that taking a 75 or 100mg aspirin on the day of travel makes any difference, some experts still recommend it.

If you've previously had a DVT or a pulmonary embolism, you'll need an injection of low-molecular-weight heparin (LMWH, with various brand names) before the flight. Talk to your doctor about this.

Finally, if you get pain or swelling in a leg or sudden chest pain any time up to several weeks after a flight, go to a doctor straight away.

Jet Lag

Nearly all long flights make you feel tired, especially if you miss sleep. But flights longer than about five hours that cross time zones also throw out your body clock, producing jet lag. Some people suffer jet lag more severely than others. Each person has to to develop his or her own coping mechanisms, but here are some tips that help some people.

• Be as well rested as possible before departure, getting a good night's sleep before you leave.
• Try to arrive at your destination in the evening.
• Take short naps during the flight, helped by ear plugs and eye shades.
• Eat light meals, and avoid coffee and alcohol.
• Consider breaking your flight for 24 hours.
• The correct use of light can help. For westward flights, try to stay awake at your destination while it is light, after a short nap if you arrive early in the morning. After flying east, avoid bright light in the morning but be outdoors in the afternoon.
• Try melatonin, the body's own sleeping pill. One way to use this is to take 2–5mg at bedtime on the day you arrive and for

several days afterwards. It's hard to get good-quality products, but the US and Hong Kong are two places where it's available.
• If you have something very important to do when you get off the plane, try to arrive a day early so your body can start to adapt and you can catch up on sleep.

Travel Sickness

During smooth flights, travel sickness is not usually a problem, but it can be very different when there is a lot of turbulence. If you have a tendency to get travel sick or have had problems on a previous flight, try anti-sickness pills such as cinnarizine (Stugeron) 15mg or promethazine (Avomine) 25mg, at least two hours before the flight. These also work for other forms of travel sickness, including seasickness. An alternative is a scopolamine skin patch (Transderm Scop).

Trouble Sleeping

It's best not to use sleeping pills on a plane unless it's really necessary, because sleeping in a cramped position for too long increases the risk of DVT. But if you just can't drop off naturally or really need to be well rested at the other end, try a short-acting sleeping pill, which normally has to be prescribed by a doctor. Good ones are zopiclone 3.75mg or 7.5mg, zaleplon 5mg or 10mg, or zolpidem 5mg. These can also be used for a night or two after you arrive.

> **Seating tip**
>
> Booking a seat in the middle of the plane and in a central block of seats can help reduce travel sickness, as there is less pitching and rolling; the same applies in boats.

Am I Allowed to Fly?

After some illnesses or operations you may not be allowed to fly for a certain period. Whether or not you're fit to fly is mainly a matter of common sense and knowing yourself, plus of course advice from a doctor. But most international carriers also give guidelines – see your airline's website for details.

TRAVELLING BY SEA: CRUISE SHIPS

More than 10 million people a year cruise the world's seas and oceans. The commonest destinations are the Mediterranean and Caribbean, but worldwide cruises are increasingly popular. Despite media reports of health problems on cruise ships, the great majority of passengers have an enjoyable and illness-free trip. However, there are some special health precautions you should follow if this is how you plan to spend your next holiday, or if you get a job working on a cruise ship.

If you have any pre-existing health problems, have a check-up from your doctor before you book. Although there are good-quality health facilities on the larger cruise ships, who wants to become seriously ill far from land?

Get the recommended vaccinations for all your ports of call

A less serious, if common, problem is sea sickness. Follow the advice on page 44 and the instructions you will be given on board in case of bad weather.

Vaccinations

Have all the travel jabs recommended for your age, and in addition those recommended for any port or country that you visit en route, especially if staying overnight. Diseases to be covered include influenza for all those over 65 or who are recommended to have this jab because of other health conditions *(see page 29)*. This needs to be the latest flu vaccine recommended by the World Health Organization for whichever hemisphere you are travelling in. Flu can spread very rapidly on cruise ships, so an increasing number of healthy travellers also have a flu jab if travelling in winter months. A single pneumococcal vaccine is recommended for all those over 65 or who have a similar risk to those recommended flu jabs.

Diarrhoea

Diarrhoea caused by a variety of organisms is very common on cruise ships. Probably the commonest and the one that causes greatest havoc is norovirus, previously known as Norwalk-Like Virus (NLV). Although usually not serious, this virus causes profuse diarrhoea and vomiting after an incubation period of 24 to 48 hours. It spreads rapidly through ships and in other places where crowds gather together for any length of time. You can do a great deal to prevent it by being very strict with food and water hygiene, and by washing your hands very frequently, and always before eating or after going to the toilet. Experts recommend that you wash thoroughly for 20 seconds with soap and water. If that is not possible, use alcohol wipes containing at least 60 percent alcohol. With norovirus the infection also spreads through contaminated surfaces, so being an obsessional hand-washer could be a bonus.

Before signing up for a cruise, ask carefully about how closely the boat follows international health and safety regulations and the details of any outbreaks that have occurred on your chosen ship in the past two years. Ask what precautions they use to minimise the risk of norovirus. For example, some companies will ask anyone with gastroenteritis to be confined to their cabins for 48 hours, the best way to avoid spreading the virus. Of course, even if the ship has a good record, there is nothing to prevent a highly infectious passenger embarking en route and spreading the disease.

The majority of cruise passengers enjoy illness-free trips

SURVIVAL WHEN AWAY

SOME GENERAL TIPS

• Keep a personal health list with you, including: medicines you normally take, antimalarials you're on, allergies, past or serious health problems, a copy of your health insurance, and your insurance policy's Emergency Helpline Number.

• Tell your travelling companion or a first-aider if you're ill. This is especially important with malaria.

• Find out the name and address of a good hospital and doctor when you first arrive in a place, especially if you're travelling independently. When in a remote place, know the hospital or doctor you would try to reach in a medical emergency and how to get there.

• If you have to go to hospital, ask someone to accompany you; hospitals can be frightening or bewildering places, especially if you're ill and don't speak the language. Equally, be prepared to go with someone you know who needs medical care.

• Don't accept a blood transfusion, unless it comes from a reliable and trustworthy friend or contact with a compatible blood group or unless other forms of intravenous fluid are not doing the job. In a resource-poor country do not accept a transfusion from an unknown source or give permission on behalf of a seriously ill friend unless the doctor thinks it's absolutely essential to save life.

• Don't believe a negative malaria test if you have been at risk and continue to be ill with serious symptoms. Self-treat but remain under the best medical care you can.

• Check that any medicines you take are made by a reputable company, preferably a multinational. Fake drugs are very common in developing countries. Check the expiry date and the generic (scientific) name as well as the local brand name, to make sure it is the right medicine to use.

• Avoid preparations by mouth that contain steroids unless you know these are what you need. They are over-prescribed in many countries and can cause a variety of side effects.

• Because of the possibility of contamination, avoid blood- or serum-based products unless they are from a developed-country source.

• Avoid having injections, and above all intravenous fluids, unless you are seriously unwell and cannot take medicines or fluids by mouth. A friend may need to help explain this on your behalf. If you do need an injection, ask the hospital to use your own sterile needle and syringe, unless you are very confident about the quality of the clinic or hospital.

A choice of practitioners

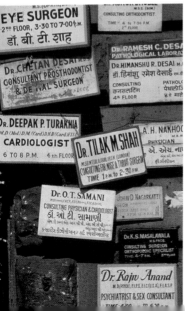

Medical Care Abroad

• Don't assume that the health-care system is similar to the one you left at home.

• Seek out medical units that have a reputation for caring for foreigners.

• Clarify payment issues from the start.

• Understand that in some cultures questions from patient or family are seen as challenges to authority.

• Have exit strategies that allow you to bow out gracefully from local providers if you are dissatisfied.

• Watch out for unethical doctors who may invade your personal privacy unnecessarily.

Question: What's often more common in travellers than diarrhoea? Answer: Constipation. Read about that fascinating subject on page 60, but first…

DIARRHOEA

Call it the trots, the runs, Delhi Belly, Pharaoh's or Montezuma's Revenge or the Aztec Quickstep, the effects are the same: gripes and gloom. You have a one in two chance of getting traveller's diarrhoea during a two-week holiday in a developing country. Whether you come down with diarrhoea depends on where you travel to, how long you're there and what you do. Taking the right precautions reduces your chances of getting a dose of the trots.

What to Avoid

Apart from avoiding the foods listed below, an important precaution is to eat only in restaurants known to have an excellent reputation. This is not always easy to ascertain, but it's still worth asking around. In the best resorts in common tourist destinations there are usually good levels of hygiene, but if you're in an any doubt it's better to be safe than sorry.

• Water – unboiled, unfiltered, unsterilised.
• Milk – unless you've boiled it or it's been added to a cauldron of bubbling tea, chai or whatever.
• Salads – unless you're in a resort with known high standards of hygiene or you've prepared salads at home, washing them with clean, preferably iodised or chlorinated, water (using a concentration three times stronger than that used to make drinking water safe).

If you are travelling to remote areas where boiling
water is not an option, a
portable water purifier
produces safe drinking
water from any available
source. Iodine resin water
purifiers physically filter
water through an activated
charcoal cloth. The iodine
then chemically disinfects
the water making it safe to
drink. Other types of water
purifiers use ceramic filters
impregnated with silver.

- Uncooked vegetables or unpeeled fruit – unless carefully home-prepared.
- Reheated food – especially meat and rice.
- Ice and ice cream.
- Cheese – usually. It can be a disaster.
- Cold food – especially if left uncovered to attract nature's specialised germ carriers: flies.
- Shellfish.
- Uncooked or inadequately cooked eggs – when safe to eat, the yolk should be hard.
- Cocktails and freshly made fruit juice.
- Cold sauces and toppings.

What's Safe

There's a lot you can safely eat and drink, and there's no need to lust continually after the favourite dish you ate at home. Your mantra should be: 'Cook it, peel it, clean it or forget it.' Here are the food and drinks that are usually safe to have.

- Any food recently cooked and served hot.
- Food you've carefully prepared at home – unless your cooking skills or those of your friends are very inadequate.
- Fruit and vegetables – ideally cooked, or washed then peeled.
- Water or milk that has been boiling for one minute, or for three minutes if you're over 2,000m (6,500ft) in elevation.
- Tea, coffee and other drinks made with water that has boiled.
- Fizzy drinks with sealed tops – but only bottled water if top and bottle seem to match or the local intelligentsia say

they're safe. There's a lot of recycled bug-laden water dressed up in smart bottles, so be wary. If in doubt, drop in an iodine or chlorine tablet 20 minutes or more before drinking.
• Most tinned foods.

Danger Zones

Hospitality. The chief, bishop or your future mother-in-law offers you a plateful from What to Avoid *(see pages 51–2)*. Smile, help yourself to what you decide is safest, dabble and play with your food, apologise that you have a weak stomach or you started a fast earlier that day. 'We're not allowed to eat that in our tribe/culture.' If you have your own personal ploy please use it. You have two priorities – not offending your stomach and not offending your host, usually in that order. Of course, some local delicacies may not look very appetising but are quite safe to eat. Why not try those fried locusts or flying ants?

It's best to peel your own fruit

Your hands and fingernails. Wash your hands with soap and water after going to the toilet, after touching animals, cleaning babies and before eating or preparing food. An alternative to soap and water is antibacterial cleaning gel containing up to 60 percent alcohol. It's also advisable to keep your fingernails short and clean.

Your own cooking set-up. When you don't really bother about the following things, you've got a problem:

• A really clean, tidy kitchen.
• Regularly wiping clean any surface used for preparing food.
• No scraps lying around.
• Not using a floor cloth to wipe the table.
• Fridge kept spotless.
• Never letting raw meat drip on or contaminate other food.
• Only preparing food with really clean hands and utensils.
• Rat-catching and cockroach-bashing.
• Making sure there's no standing water near the house.
• Frequently disposing of rubbish.

Treatment

If you're unlucky enough to have an attack of diarrhoea, perhaps accompanied by vomiting, here's how to limit the damage. Check out <www.rehydrate.org>.

Keep up the fluids. You could use oral rehydration salts (always have with you a few packets, such as Dioralyte), make your own rehydration solution *(see left)*, or use a carbonated drink, such as Sprite or Seven-Up, defizzed by some

> ### Oral rehydration
>
> A do-it-yourself oral rehydration solution, recommended by the World Health Organization: add eight level teaspoons of sugar and one level teaspoon of salt to 1 litre of safe, preferably boiled, drinking water.

Food is safest when freshly prepared

gentle shaking (don't drink beer until you're better). Some prefer soup or tea. Whatever you use, aim for two glasses each time you go to the toilet, one for children. Drink it slowly.

Take some loperamide (Imodium). Especially if you're in danger of losing control of your bowels, or the bus is leaving in an hour. This medication blocks but doesn't cure. However, it does help to prevent dehydration. The adult dose: take two capsules or tablets, then one every six hours if your motions continue loose. Pregnant women should not use loperamide. And don't use it in cases of bloody diarrhoea or dysentery, or when you have a fever over 38.5°C (101°F).

Bad bout or getting worse? If you have more than five stools in 24 hours, have a fever or pass blood in your stools you should seek medical advice. You can also take some ciprofloxacin (adult dose 500mg daily), for one to three days (one day if symptoms are relatively mild, extending up to three if they are more severe or you are passing blood). Cipro

Medicine abroad

Note that most of the medicines mentioned in this section are prescription-only in the UK. They can often be bought over the counter in developing countries, but be aware of counterfeit or poor-quality drugs and those beyond their expiry date. It's usually better to see a doctor or health worker rather than to self-diagnose and self-treat.

works in more than half of all cases of traveller's trots. Don't use it in pregnancy, and not if you're under 16 (it might harm cartilages). An alternative is azithromycin: normal adult dose 1,000mg once, or 500mg daily for three days. It is safe to use in pregnancy, and in children at the correct dose for age.

See a doctor or experienced health worker if you continue to vomit, you are seriously dehydrated, you have bloody diarrhoea and/or fever (you could have dysentery), or things don't improve (see below). Also, children should get medical attention if symptoms are serious.

Groaning beyond a week. Doctors call this chronic diarrhoea. See a doctor and try to get a stool test, especially if there's blood or slime in your stool, or your weight is falling.

Diarrhoea Specials

Diarrhoea can be a symptom of a serious infection. Watch out for the following.

Giardia

Technically *giardiasis* caused by Giardia duodenalis (lamblia).

How do you get this? By eating unwashed salads, drinking unclean water and from ignoring all the sensible precautions listed on pages 51–4. Giardia is especially common in those eating, drinking or swimming in areas with poor sanitation. It is found almost worldwide, but in practice is usually caught in developing countries. Infection can also occur when trekkers, wilderness campers and other outdoor enthusiasts drink from contaminated streams. All water, however clean it appears, should be boiled or purified before consumption *(see page 52)*.

What's it like? Smelly wind (gas), smelly burps, or just an upset stomach and lots of wind. You may also have a poor appetite, and be losing weight and losing energy.

What do you do about it? Easy! Up your personal hygiene and take tinidazole (Fasigyn) 500mg tablets, four taken together (not if pregnant or breastfeeding). Re-

Boil water to sterilise it

peat again after two weeks. However, it's better to get a stool test to confirm it first, providing the lab is reliable.

Amoebas

Technically *amoebiasis* caused by Entamoeba histolytica.

How do you get this? In just about the same way as Giardia and other forms of diarrhoea. Again, it's found almost worldwide, but budget travellers in developing countries are probably at greatest risk.

What's it like? It gives you diarrhoea, sometimes with blood, often with mucus. You may have a mild fever and be trotting to the toilet, but rarely more than five or six times a day.

The main danger is that germs can occasionally move up-stream to the liver and blow up into an abscess. It's usually obvious when amoebas migrate – you feel awful, have a painful liver (below your ribs on the right) and have a swinging fever. This spells 'see a doctor immediately'.

What do you do about it? For amoebas that are confined to your bowels, the treatment is either tinidazole 500mg tablets, four daily all taken at once for three days, or metronidazole (Flagyl) 800mg three times daily for five days. Both these medicines, but especially the latter, can make you feel sick and wretched, and mixing alcohol with the pills might remind you of a major hangover.

Mistaken identity

Lots of people incorrectly blame their troubled insides on amoebas. One reason: amoebiasis is over-diagnosed by labs because its cause (Entamoeba histolytica) and the far commoner but innocent amoeba (E. dispar) look just the same under the microscope, but labs usually report both as E. histolytica.

Ideally you should follow the treatment above by taking diloxanide furoate (Furamide) 500mg tablets, one tablet three times daily for 10 days (these tablets can be hard to get hold of). This gets rid of amoebic cysts, which can remain dormant inside you after all the symptoms have disappeared.

Bacillary Dysentery
Sounds awful, looks awful, is awful.

What's it like? This is the dreaded infection when you squit endlessly, usually with blood, often with high fever, and wonder if you'll survive until tomorrow. It's almost part of the adventure traveller's initiation, but it's largely preventable if you follow the rules above about clean food and water.

Clean crockery reduces risk of contamination

What do you do about it? Plenty to drink, moral support from an experienced friend and ciprofloxacin 500mg daily for three days *(see pages 55–6)*. See a doctor as soon as possible unless the medicine works very rapidly.

Cholera

This disease is extremely rare in travellers. The most likely place to pick it up is South Asia. Front-line aid workers face the greatest risk of infection.

What's it like? Usually it gives you severe watery diarrhoea that looks like rice water. It's common to feel sick or to vomit. You become quickly dehydrated. Other commoner types of diarrhoea can give you similar symptoms.

What do you do about it? The first thing is to start oral rehydration immediately, as much as you can manage, but start by drinking it slowly *(see pages 54–5)*. Then take either doxycycline 100mg, three together, or ciprofloxacin 1,000mg or azithromycin 1,000mg as a one-off dose. See a doctor.

Typhoid Fever
Typhoid fever can cause diarrhoea. For more information, see pages 97–8.

CONSTIPATION

Why do our insides sometimes turn into concrete? There are various reasons:

• We don't drink enough and so we get dehydrated.
• When we need to go to the toilet there isn't the opportunity, or we don't fancy the only ones available, so we suppress what doctors describe as 'the call to stool'. It's one call we shouldn't ignore.
• We cut down on the fruit and veg because there isn't any, or we're scared it may give us the runs.
• We took too much Imodium.
• We've changed time zones.
• We're just one of those people who get constipated.

Treatment
• Have plenty to drink.
• Eat fruit and veg daily.
• Go to the toilet when you can and the opportunity is there.
• Take Senakot or an equivalent laxative – one or two at night until your bowels unblock.
• Be patient: take less Imodium when you next have diarrhoea.
• If things are desparate, self-treat with glycerine supposi-tories, which are widely available.
• Don't worry that it will cause your intestines irretrievable harm. Some people only go once or twice a week anyway.

MALARIA

Malaria is caused by a single-celled organism, a Plasmodium, which enters the blood stream and affects various organs in the body. It is spread by the bites of the female Anopheles mosquito. There are two main types of malaria. The commonest and most serious is caused by Plasmodium falciparum; this is the one that can cause cerebral malaria. The other is so-called benign malaria, rarely fatal but still a nuisance and sometimes recurring for months when you leave an affected area. The map on page 11 shows you where the disease is found.

A happy hunting ground for
Ms Anopheles

Malaria is a serious risk and, along with road accidents, is the most likely thing to give you big trouble on your travels. If you're going to a malarious area, be sure to get expert advice and consult further information, such as another reliable book or website *(see pages 141–2)*. Assume that the Anopheles mosquito has a higher IQ than you.

Symptoms
Usually a bad headache, sweats and shivers, bodyache, often diarrhoea or vomiting. However, your symptoms may be much less obvious. A significant fever (over 38°C/100°F) in a malaria zone is malaria until proved otherwise.

Prevention

Malaria-causing mosquitoes start biting from about one hour before sunset, and continue through the night until about one hour after dawn. They go for any unprotected skin, and they especially like the feet and ankles. Prevention is a combination of stopping these insects from biting and taking antimalaria tablets.

Clothing

Keep your body covered as much as possible. This is the main way of preventing being bitten when you are up and about. Lightweight cotton garments will help a bit, but keep in mind that determined mosquitoes can bite through a pair of socks or jeans. If you are in a high-risk zone or likely to be very exposed to bites, soak your clothes, especially socks and trousers, in Deet or spray them with permethrin.

Insect Repellent

In addition to covering up, you need to use an insect repellent, ideally containing Deet. This comes in many brands and strengths, but about 50 percent Deet is what most experts recommend. Apply it at least every four hours. If you absolutely can't or won't use Deet, the best alternative is a repellent containing extract of lemon eucalyptus, or a new preparation known as Picaridin. Remember that Deet destroys plastics, varnish and synthetic fibres, but not wool, cotton or linen. It is rare for Deet to cause skin allergies in either adults or children, but it should not be used on children under two months.

Mosquito Nets

To protect you during sleeping hours or while resting in bed, use a permethrin-impregnated mosquito or bed net. Most nets come pre-soaked in permethrin or a similar insecticide, but make sure. For long-term travellers, nets need re-soaking,

Mosquitoes go for unprotected skin

usually every six months. Remember to tuck the net in very carefully and make sure there are no holes in it.

Malaria-Prevention Tablets

You must take malaria-prevention tablets, known as anti-malarials or malaria prophylactics. Which antimalarials you take will depend on your travel plans, so if you are heading to a malarious area, get expert advice from a nurse or doctor who knows about travel medicine, taking into account where you will be going, how long for, and what you will be doing.

For full details about antimalarials, see pages 34–8. Briefly, the best three choices for most malarious areas, including sub-Saharan Africa, are doxycycline: 100mg daily; meflo-quine (Lariam): 250mg once a week; and Malarone: one daily. Before using any of them, read through the patient in-formation leaflet. You should start taking antimalarials be-fore leaving home, but if you haven't, it's still not too late.

A net is good for protection during sleeping hours

Other Precautions

If you are living in a house, screen your windows and doors and keep them shut from before dusk until after dawn. Use a knock-down spray to kill any mosquitoes in the house. Try to eliminate breeding sites such as tall vegetation, flower pots and other containers where mosquitoes can breed (this also helps to prevent dengue fever; *see pages 92–5*).

Either at home or in a hotel, sleep in an air-conditioned room or under a ceiling fan turned up reasonably high. This reduces your chances of being bitten.

Mosquito coils and electric mosquito killers may help, but you should not rely on these alone. Still sleep under a net. Mosquito buzzers don't work.

Treatment

1. Act on symptoms. If you suspect malaria, see the best health worker you can as soon as possible, and get a malaria blood test.

2. If this test is positive, get treated immediately. It is often best to use the standby treatment you may have with you, because effective drugs may not be available locally. See The Best Treatments below.

3. If the blood test is negative and you still feel ill, self-treat anyway, because many blood tests are inaccurate, and you can still have malaria even if the test is negative, especially if the test was taken at a time when you didn't have a fever.

4. Keep yourself under the watchful eye of a doctor or trusted health worker until you're feeling OK.

The Best Treatments

You could take these medications with you from home as standby treatment kits *(see page 34)* or use ones bought locally if the quality of supplies is reliable and the medications are within their expiry dates.

Co-artemether (Co-artem, Riamet). This contains artemether 20mg and lumefantrine 120mg. The adult dose, which should be taken with food if possible, is four tablets to start with then four more at 8, 24, 36, 48 and 60 hours, a total of 24 tablets. Side effects are usually minor. It is best not used in pregnancy or when breastfeeding.

Malarone. These tablets contain atovaquone 250mg and proguanil 100mg. The adult dose is four tablets taken together for three days, a total of 12 tablets. Side effects are usually minor. It's best not used when pregnant or breastfeeding very young infants. Ideally, use another treatment if you are using Malarone as a prophylactic.

Quinine and doxycycline. The adult dose of quinine is 300mg tablets, two together every eight hours for three days plus, starting at the same time, doxycycline

Don't stop now!

If you stop taking anti-malarials too soon, you may contract malaria. Take those tablets to the bitter end!

Coils also help to keep mosquitos at bay

100mg twice daily for seven days. Side effects (from quinine) include ringing in the ears and nausea. In pregnancy quinine alone can be used, but for five days.

Many other treatments are used in developing countries, only some of which are effective, so whenever possible see doctors experienced in travel medicine or who are known to have a high reputation for treating travellers.

Poor Choices for Malaria Treatment

Chloroquine. This hardly works in large stretches of Africa, Southeast Asia and Amazonia.

Halofantrine (Halfan or 'Scary H'). It works well but can affect the heart – yours perhaps. Emergencies only.

Fansidar – sulfadoxine 500mg and pyrimethamine 25mg (SP). This is losing its effectiveness in much of sub-Saharan Africa, though it still works in many other malarious areas.

Special Situations

Malaria When You Get Home

You can get falciparum malaria any time up to three months and occasionally longer after leaving a malarious area; other forms may take up to a year or more to show symptoms. If you develop any symptoms (see page 61) that might be malaria within the first three months, get seen by a doctor and have a malaria blood test as soon as possible. If you are in an area where there is poor health care, self-treat as described above.

Visiting Friends and Relatives

At high risk of getting malaria are people who used to live in a malarious area, for example Africa and Asia, have emigrated to a developed country or non-malarious area, and then go back to visit friends and relatives. Immunity rapidly disappears in the first year away from malaria zones, so if this situation applies to you, take antimalarials when you visit your family and follow all the advice above.

Pregnancy

Ideally, pregnant women with no immunity to malaria should avoid living in areas with a high malaria risk. Mosquitoes are attracted to pregnant women, and dangers are greater in the last third of pregnancy both for mother and baby. If you must visit a malarious area while pregnant, lessen your risk of infection by taking mefloquine (now considered safe in pregnancy, *see pages 35–6*) and avoiding getting bitten.

Foolish Advice You Should Ignore

– Try these garlic pills; mosquitoes hate them (many don't).

– I'm depending on my homoeopathic medicines (take them if you want to, but don't rely on them).

– My friend took her antimalarials and she still got malaria (but if she hadn't taken them, her sweats and headaches would probably have been worse and she may have ended up in the local hospital).

– We're expats, experts, the guys who live here. We don't take antimalarials (unreliable advice, often wrong, especially with resistant strains spreading across the world).

– We have lived away from a malarious area for several years and are now visiting friends and relatives. We won't get malaria because we still have our natural immunity (this is untrue; most immunity fades after 6 to 12 months, and you are at high risk).

Children
Children can get seriously ill very quickly. You'll need to take the strictest precautions, including using antimalarials appropriate for children. Mefloquine can be used to prevent malaria in children who weigh 5kg (11lb) or more (that is, from about three months). Malarone can be used to prevent malaria in children who weigh 11kg (about 24lb) or more, and for treatment from 5kg, using Malarone paediatric tablets. Follow dosage charts carefully.

RABIES

This viral infection is rare among travellers, but always fatal. It's caused by a bite, scratch or lick from an infected mammal, usually a dog, sometimes a cat, monkey or bat. Mammals may not show any symptoms, even when they are very infectious, so a normally behaved dog may still have rabies.

By far the most affected regions are South Asia and Africa. On the bright side, there are more than 50 countries where rabies can't get you.

Symptoms
Typical symptoms of rabies are fever, severe headache, bouts of terror, and paralysis followed by death.

Prevention

This fearsome disease is completely preventable by following the basic rules on immunisation and avoidance of animals.

Immunisation

At least a month before you travel, talk about risk/benefit with a travel health adviser *(see page 30)*. Three jabs are usually needed, though some clinics use two. They are simple and largely painless. Forget all those stories about horrible needles into the stomach wall – that's only if you get gobbled up in the real back of beyond and haven't had your pre-travel jabs.

One thing to remember. The pre-travel injections still leave you with a tiny chance of getting infected after a bite. But having had the pre-travel jabs gives you a day or two to get help if you get bitten and you only need two more injections rather than the rabies immunoglobulin injection.

Avoid Animals

Playing with, touching, kissing or annoying any furry mammal – be it dog, cat, monkey, racoon, mongoose or polar bear – is a no-no. Avoiding animals may be hard for youngsters,

Rabies: What Not to Do

Don't get into a frenzy and start emailing friends and doctors so that everyone joins in the panic. Just follow the procedures and relax. If you are still anxious, make a phone call to or email any well-informed doctor you know at home or elsewhere.

Don't believe anyone who says all you need to do is take some tablets and come back in a week.

Bites get infected easily, so don't ignore this possibility; see a doctor, and start antibiotics, ideally co-amoxiclav, if there's any sign of infection. Are you up to date with tetanus? If not, have a booster *(see page 28)*.

so if you're travelling with children, keep a close watch on them. They (and you) can have a low-risk cuddle with friends' pets that have had their full anti-rabies jabs.

Treatment

1. Wash the wound carefully with soap and water – making sure you remove all saliva and dirt. Apply some iodine solution or alcohol: gin from your hip flask will do. Don't scrub and don't have any gaping wound stitched – at least not until you've seen the best doctor in town.

2. Assume that the dog, cat or monkey is rabid if it's behaving strangely, it's unknown, or it disappears and you can't trace it. Remember many rabid animals behave entirely normally. If the animal is still alive after 10 days, you're in the clear, and can stop the jabs.

3. Start injections. You'll be in one of two categories.

Category 1

If you've had a full course of rabies jabs within three years prior to being bitten or you have had an original course of three and boosters at least every five years since, you should have two more rabies shots like the ones you had before leaving. These will have been Human Diploid Cell Strain Vaccine (HDCV or HDCSV), or Purified Duck Embryo Vaccine (PDEV), or Purified Vero Cell Vaccine (PVRV), or Purified Chicken Embryo Cell Vaccine (PCECV), or RVA. These five types are largely interchangeable. Most also have trade names, for example Rabipur, which is widely available. Have the first jab as soon as possible and the other three days later.

Category 2

If you're not in the first category or you're not sure, then you're in this category. You will need to have a full course of five jabs of any of the types listed above: one jab immediately, the others on days 3, 7, 14 and about 28. And if the animal has broken the skin, or licked broken skin, you'll also need some human rabies immunoglobulin as soon as possible. It's often hard to get hold of and very expensive, so this is the time to pester the hospital, embassy, consul or whoever. You will need as much as possible, a minimum of 20 units per kilogram of your body weight, carefully infiltrated into and around the bite.

AVOIDING ACCIDENTS

Roads

Road accidents don't just happen, they're caused. Some 1.2 million people die in road crashes each year, and a further 50 million are injured. For travellers, car crashes are the commonest reason for coming back home in a body bag or being medically evacuated.

That's a pretty direct way to put it, but people need to be realistic about so-called accidents. Usually there's a fool be-

Vehicles aren't the only danger on the roads

hind one or both steering wheels or in the buffalo cart, or crossing the road. Of course, it may be you. So what are the secrets of keeping safe?

First, be very careful as a pedestrian. More pedestrians die in car crashes than those inside cars. Some other tips:

• Fit and wear seat belts, in both front and back seats. It won't always be possible, but when it is possible, do it.
• Make sure the vehicle you usually drive is kept in really good shape, especially the brakes, steering, tyres and lights.
• Don't ever get behind the wheel when: you are really tired; for long periods without a break; overnight unless there's absolutely no other option; without adequate headlights; you've been drinking or taking drugs; you don't have a co-driver or someone to crack jokes or sing with to keep you awake; you have to break the land-speed record between Timbuktu and Nairobi to be on time to meet Mr Important.

• Be choosy about your mode of transport. Yes, impossible sometimes, but you can get to know or recognise the most reliable buses. Try to avoid rickshaws, matatus and pick-ups.

• Try never to join the swaying masses on the back of any pick-up or lorry.

• Wear a helmet whenever you're on a motorbike – even for 100m (100yds) – and when you're on a bicycle.

• Beware of unlit vehicles at night, especially if stationary or slow-moving.

• Assume other road users are idiots and make allowances.

• If you are a passenger and feel the driver is not in control, be bold and ask him or her to slow down. If the driver won't, ask to get out (but choose an appropriate, safe area to do this). Your boldness might save lives, including your own.

• In your own vehicle always carry a torch, warning triangle, first-aid kit and leather gloves for pulling victims free.

In the Water

Avoid swimming accidents by following these guidelines:

• Don't drink alcohol and swim.

• Be careful around the slippery edges of swimming pools.

• Check out the depth of the pool before diving in: penalty for forgetting is a broken neck.

• Don't go out of your depth. Assume that you're a slightly worse swimmer than you want your friends to think.

• At the beach, always swim with a companion unless you are very familiar with the beach.

• Listen to what the locals have to say – about currents, crocs, sharks, box jellyfish and stingrays.

In case of emergency

• Avoid swimming in polluted waters or if there's any smell of sewage. Make sure swimming pools look and smell clean, preferably of chlorine.
• Wear a life-jacket for off-shore water sports, when using boats of any kind – inflatables, canoes, rafts or sailing boats.
• Remember lakes in sub-Saharan Africa can give you bilharzia *(see pages 90–2)*, especially Lake Malawi.
• Keep a special watch on kids and don't forget sun protection for them – and for you.

Hotels and Home Territory
The following precautions apply anywhere, but especially when you're living or travelling in a new place or where everything seems very different from what you're used to.

• Take care on hotel balconies; some are flimsily built.
• Avoid dodgy electrics – bare wires, and shower-heads touching the mains. In showers that you don't trust, wear rubber-soled flip-flops.
• Be on the lookout for walls and windows, steep paths and all sorts of places where children of all ages can get stuck, get hit, slip or fall off. Do a risk assessment of anywhere you'll be living or working, to locate obvious or lurking dangers.
• Take extra care crossing the road, especially if cars are driving on the side of the road you're not used to, the traffic is chaotic, or you've come from up-country or feel jet lagged.

SEX, SENSE AND HIV

There are about 20 sexually transmitted infections (STIs), including the worst of the bunch, hepatitis B and HIV. In 2006, 40 million people were living with HIV, and 8,000 die from AIDS every day. Five million new cases of HIV were reported in 2006, with over 60 percent of these in Africa, but no part of the world is safe. South and Southeast Asia, Eastern Europe and Russia have increasing levels of HIV infection. Of course we all know about HIV. Or do we?

HIV

HIV, or human immunodeficiency virus, if left untreated eventually leads to AIDS, which is usually fatal. It's generally not possible to see any signs that a person is infected. After catching HIV, a person becomes infectious a short time later, although it takes up to three and occasionally six months before the standard HIV tests shows a positive result. Antiretroviral drugs (ARVs, ART, HAART) can control HIV, and most people can live fully productive lives with few symptoms. If you do get infected, it is vital to make sure you have good medical care and take ARVs if recommended.

How HIV is Spread

The commonest way of catching HIV is by having vaginal, anal or oral sex with an infected partner. Your partner may not know if they have HIV, or may deny it and will probably seem quite healthy. Other ways in which HIV is spread are:

• Infected blood transfusions.
• Dirty needles, tattoos, body-piercing kit, barbers.
• Occasionally from dentists or through sharing a toothbrush with someone who is HIV positive.
• Occasionally through infected blood (and some other body fluids) getting onto chapped or broken skin.
• From mother to child at birth or through breastfeeding.

Prevention

• Decide to abstain from casual sexual encounters. The only way of being sure to avoid HIV or any STI is for complete mutual loyalty between partners both known to be HIV negative (and free from a sexually transmitted infection).
• Take condoms with you and use them every time, unless you are sure your principles will guarantee abstinence from casual sex, even at moments of stress or loneliness. A condom reduces your risk but does not remove it altogether. However, always using a condom and always using it correctly is absolutely essential if you have sex with someone who is not definitely HIV negative. And it also greatly reduces your risk of picking up other STIs.
• Know your blood group if going for any length of time or off the beaten track.

- Take a needle and syringe kit – and some intravenous fluid and a drip-set if you'll be backpacking or roughing it in HIV danger zones *(see page 75)*.
- Women should avoid situations, lifestyle and types of dress which encourage the unwanted attentions of men.
- Avoid accidents *(see page 71)*. Being in an accident is the most likely cause of needing blood transfusions, operations and needles.
- Avoid blood transfusions, except from a safe source, unless you're likely to die. This is the time when your friends may need to make that decision – or you may

Stay safe

need to on a friend's behalf. If you must have a transfusion, receive blood from the most reliable friend available who has a compatible group. (This is the main reason for knowing your blood group.)

Treatment

You're back home now; your resolutions didn't work (or you didn't make any) and you're scared you've caught HIV, even though you expect it's a slim chance. Get some HIV counselling and have an HIV test. You'll find out the result in just a few days. For a reliable result, you have to wait 90 days after your last encounter under the palm trees or that reluctant visit to a clinic when you left behind your needle and syringe kit.

Other STIs

Hepatitis B (which is 100 times more infectious than HIV), genital herpes (which may persist for years), gonorrhoea, chlamydia (which may cause few or no symptoms until much later), syphilis and other STIs are increasingly common. If you think you may have an STI (especially if you have had a urethral discharge or ulcers in the genital area), have a check-up at a genito-urinary medicine (GUM) clinic or other appropriate clinic or specialist as soon as you have access to good health care. Get checked even if you have no symptoms but you know you have put yourself at risk.

ALCOHOL AND DRUGS

Too much alcohol, or any drugs, are private and public enemy number one for many travellers. Private, because they do you real harm; public, because they cause a risk to others, such as making it more likely you will crash a car, and because being under their influence can cause offence in many cultures.

Most of us may want to try the local home-brew (in many countries a bad idea because of unknown contaminants), have a few beers or sample the local wine. But getting drunk, binge drinking and abusing drugs greatly increase the risk of accidents, being burgled, losing your credibility and/or catching HIV or another STI. Best rule: maximum 21 units in a week, maximum 3 units in an evening. If you are in a culture in which alcohol is banned or considered a social evil, for example among Islamic friends or many Church groups in developing countries, it is really offensive to drink at all.

Shade can be in short supply

CLIMATE AND ALTITUDE

Too Much Sun

'Where's your sun tan?' is about the most annoying thing many white travellers are asked when they get home. It's OK to get a tan, and a certain amount of sun is good for most of us, but in the tropics and ozone-depleted climes caution is the name of the game, especially if you're fair or freckly, or taking doxycycline as an antimalarial. The ultraviolet radiation in sunlight causes sunburn, accelerated ageing of the skin and an increased risk of skin cancer.

Prevention

• Avoid being out in the sun between 10am and 3pm.
• Take extra care at a high altitude. Ultraviolet light is much stronger in the mountains, and also near or in water, sand, sea, snow or ice, which greatly add to the risk through reflection.

• Take it easy to start with: 15 minutes the first day and gradually increase, so that you tan and don't go red, and your skin
never feels sore.

• Use suncream. Go for a factor 25 or above if you're fair and
freckly, and around 15 or so if you're brown or bronze. Use
it frequently, every hour or two if you're swimming, sweating or exercising, but remember it's not as good as getting into
the shade. Deet-based insect repellents reduce the effectiveness of suncream, in which case use a cream with a higher
sun-protection factor. Apply suncream before insect repellent.

• If you're going to be active in the sun – walking, snor-
kelling, building, jogging – take extra care. A hat, sunglasses,
lip salve, umbrellas and headscarves, in addition to suncream, are useful accessories.

• If you're taking doxycycline for malaria, acne or bubonic
plague, take extra precautions – this and other tetracyclines can
make your skin burn more easily, in a minority seriously so.

• Think ahead. One of the commonest reasons for serious
sunburn is getting caught in the sun when you weren't ex-
pecting it – on a trip to a village, invited out by friends, rid-
ing in an open vehicle, going out in a boat. Always have
suncream with you, and wear sensible clothes and a hat.

Treatment

Take aspirin or paracetamol, rest and apply calamine lotion to the burnt areas. When you get home, consider having a mole check. Doctors worry about moles that bleed, ooze or itch – also ones that become larger, less regular or darker. Get familiar with your skin and report any moles or unfamiliar marks or patches, especially if they persist. Get a partner or friend to check your back or other hard-to-see places.

Too Hot

You're almost bound to overheat in the tropics, but it's worth doing everything you can to prevent this. Too much heat can leave you with heat exhaustion, which is quite common and relatively easy to treat, or the much more serious heatstroke (sunstroke), when your body mechanisms fail to cope and your temperature spirals upwards: this is an emergency. Normal body temperature is 37°C (98.6°F), but it's often lower.

Types of Heat Injury

Heat exhaustion

Symptoms – weak, exhausted, poor concentration, thirst, headache, possibly muscle cramps.

Skin – flushed, moist.

Temperature – normal or slightly raised.

Pulse – normal or slightly raised.

Heatstroke

Symptoms – confused, drowsy, vomiting, sometimes convulsions, may lead to coma.

Skin – hot, usually dry.

Temperature – high, usually above 39°C (102°F).

Pulse – fast, eg 100 per minute or above.

Keep up the fluids!

Get into the habit of drinking plenty of fluids (enough to keep your urine pale); that's a lot more than you expect – sometimes up to 12 litres (21 pints) a day in a very hot climate, as opposed to 2–2.5 litres (4–4½ pints) in a cool climate. Thirst is not an accurate sign of how much fluid you need, and you can be seriously dehydrated without feeling thirsty.

Prevention

• Take time to adapt: 14 to 21 days, usually more if you are overweight.

• Add extra salt to your food.

• Wear cotton, pale or white in colour, loose-fitting clothing, and a hat in the sun.

• Consider taking or making oral rehydration solution (ORS) when it's very hot or humid, or you develop even mild diarrhoea *(see page 54)*.

• Don't exercise in the sun or the heat of the day.

• Avoid excessive alcohol and all recreational drugs, especially Ecstasy.

Treatment

• Get into the shade, wearing the minimum of clothes.

• Fan vigorously, sponging body with a cool, wet cloth.

• Drink as much as possible without causing nausea – soft, uncarbonated drinks or ORS are best (more slowly if nauseated), at the rate of up to 2 litres (4 pints) an hour until urine is pale.

• Monitor body temperature to ensure it is falling.

• Get immediate medical care if not improving, consciousness is impaired or temperature is not coming down.

• Don't forget that malaria can mimic heatstroke or be part of its cause.

Too Cold

Problems with the cold don't only occur in the obvious cold-weather areas, but can happen in the tropics if the altitude is great enough. Three factors go to make a dangerous mix: a cold environment (usually at high altitude), wind and being wet. Hypothermia, when the core body temperature drops to below 35°C (95°F), can occur very rapidly. Anyone is at risk, thin young men, children and the elderly probably more so than most. The warning signs of hypothermia are:

• Feelings of intense cold, and uncontrollable shivering.
• An exhausted staggering gait, resembling drunkenness.
• Confused or angry responses.
• During sleep – it's only too easy to become seriously cold without you or anyone else realising it.

Falling in could be fatal

Prevention

In addition to the preventative measures listed below, in cold areas beware of dehydration: it easily occurs without you noticing it, so have plenty to drink. And don't forget goggles to prevent snow-blindness.

• Use common sense and forward thinking and planning.
• Wear plenty of clothes in the form of several layers of loose-fitting clothing. Cover your head, ears and neck; wear mittens.
• Keep dry by wearing a waterproof.
• Avoid alcohol.
• When climbing or in freezing environments, set up a buddy system, in which two of you agree to keep an eye on each other and watch for early signs of hypothermia.

Treatment

Treatment of hypothermia can be summarised as immediate, sustained rewarming.

• Remove the affected person from wind and wet, take off all wet clothes, and administer warm sugary drinks.
• Increase body warmth by sharing it with a companion in a sleeping bag or using carefully wrapped heat packs, taking care to avoid burning the skin.
• Use a warm bath where available with the temperature kept at about 40°C (104°F).
• Don't administer alcohol.
• Observe the person for 24 hours. Unless there is complete recovery and no signs of frostbite, get immediate help.

Too High

Also known as acute mountain sickness (AMS), altitude sickness can strike anyone, including the fittest. For most it occurs only at altitudes over 3,000m (about 10,000ft), the unlucky minority over 2,500m (about 8,000ft).

The symptoms usually start in the first 12 hours and include headache, loss of appetite and feeling spaced out. Other symptoms are lethargy, dry cough, nausea, dizziness, trouble sleeping, and shortness of breath on exertion.

Prevention

If possible, acclimatise for a week or so at 2,000–3,000m

Camping at altitude

(6,500–10,000ft) before going any higher, and then only climb at a reasonable pace, not sleeping more than 300m (1,000ft) higher than the night before. During the daytime you can still wield your ice-axe, but at night come down to sleep. Your motto should be: Climb high, sleep lower.

Should I take Diamox pills? Before flying into a high-altitude airport or climbing above 3,000m, consider taking azetazolamide tablets (popular name Diamox). This is a prescription-only medicine in many countries which you take in a dose of 125 or 250mg twice daily, starting two days or so before flying in high, or starting your trek from 3,000m. Keep taking them for at least two days after reaching the highest altitude. If you climb more than 300m between night stops you should certainly opt for Diamox. Give it a trial run before leaving home to make sure you're not one of the few who get side effects.

Treatment

Go down lower or don't climb any higher until the symptoms wear off. Have lots to drink. Take aspirin 600mg or paracetamol 1,000mg, or ibuprofen 400mg. If you feel nauseated, take domperidone (Motilium) 10mg or another anti-sickness pill. Have plenty to drink, including sweet, uncarbonated drinks. Avoid alcohol and sleeping tablets. Try to rest for a day.

Severe Altitude Sickness (HAPE and HACE)

Altitude sickness takes two severe forms: high altitude pulmonary oedema (HAPE) and high altitude cerebral oedema (HACE). If you have HAPE, the lungs start to swamp, making you breathless at rest, giving you bubbly or crackly breathing and a cough, often with pink frothy sputum. Your pulse rate and breathing will remain fast even at rest. You feel exhausted and sometimes your lips look blue. In HACE, the brain starts to pack up. It gets boggy with dire results: pounding headache, drowsiness, sometimes seeing things double and staggering as if you're drunk, and eventually coma. Both HAPE and HACE can be fatal.

High-Altitude Airports

If flying into any of these airports, take one or two days to rest, relax and acclimatise: Everest Base Camp, Nepal (5,500m/18,000ft), La Paz, Bolivia (4,000m/13,100ft), Juliaca by Lake Titicaca, Peru (3,800m/12,400ft), Lhasa, Tibet (3,700m/12,100), Cusco, Peru (3,300m/10,800ft), Toluca, Mexico (2,900m/9,500ft), Quito, Ecuador (2,800m/9,200ft), Aspen, Colorado (2,400m/7,800ft).

Treatment of these two conditions is simple: 'Get down that mountain fast.' Colleagues or mountain-rescue pals may have special bags like a Gamow or Certec to put you in – do what they say, but get down the hill.

Special People

People with pre-existing conditions should take extra care when planning a high-altitude trip.

• Those with heart problems. See your doctor if planning to trek above 2,500m. Angina and high blood pressure must be well controlled.
• Those with asthma. This doesn't usually get worse at high altitude, but occasionally the dry air or dust triggers it. An accompanying cold or chest infection adds appreciably to your risk.
• Children. Except for those under about three months, who should generally not sleep above about 2,500m, children have similar risks to adults. It can be hard to diagnose acute mountain sickness in very young children, for example in

The lure of the reef

those under about three years of age, because symptoms are vague, and they may not be able to explain how they feel. Get specialist advice if you plan a high-altitude family trek or holiday.
• Pregnant women. Dangers are minimal up to 3,000m. If planning to go higher than that, apart from brief stop-overs, talk to your doctor.

Too Low

Scuba diving on a coral reef can be one of the most exhilarating activities you can do. But this sport has its dangers.

Dangers of descent. If you descend too quickly or dive too deep, changes in air pressure in the ears can cause problems, including, at worst, a ruptured eardrum. Symptoms include pain, deafness and tinnitus. If any symptoms recur or persist you must see a doctor. Sinus problems can develop, especially if you have any underlying sinus infection or nasal blockage.

Dangers of ascent. These can be minimised by ascending very slowly, especially if you have been diving deep, or been submerged a long time. The most important condition is decompression sickness *(see box opposite)*. A less common condition, arterial gas embolism, when air escapes from the lung and leaks into tissues, can cause similar symptoms to decompression sickness and is treated in the same way. It is usually caused by holding your breath, and can also occur during descent.

Other health problems. The ear canal can become infected, especially after repeated dives *(see page 112)*. It's easy to sustain injuries, particularly from coral, which can be very slow to heal *(see page 107)*.

Prevention

Be physically fit. You should not dive if now or in the recent past you have had asthma or bronchitis, heart disease, cranial surgery, chronic ear and sinus disease, a severe head or neck injury, a collapsed lung, epilepsy or significant anxiety. In any case you are strongly advised to have a medical examination before diving. There are full details on this on the website of the British Diving Safety Group <www.bdsg.org>, under Resources/Medical matters.

Be well trained. You should only dive if you have been under expert instruction and received a bona fide certificate.

• Use well-checked, modern equipment.

• Dive under the supervision of an expert until you're fully confident, and always in the company of a colleague or diving buddy.

Decompression Sickness

The biggest health danger in scuba diving is decompression sickness or 'the bends', when dissolved gases come out of circulation and enter body organs. It causes a variety of symptoms: mild forms may include fatigue, headaches, painful joints, numbness and itchy skin. More severe forms may also cause severe headache, abnormal behaviour, disturbances to vision, loss of consciousness and death. Symptoms can set in up to 24 hours after a dive, but much more quickly when severe.

Decompression sickness is caused by ascending too quickly or by being too deep for too long. It can be prevented by slow ascents under expert supervision, and by avoiding long, deep dives. Treatment is through recompression in a hyperbaric chamber as soon as possible (usually available in areas where scuba diving is a major tourist activity).

Decompression sickness may occur if you fly or climb over 2,000m (6,500ft) within 12 hours of a single dive, and within 18 hours after repetitive dives or multiple days of diving.

BILHARZIA OR SCHISTOSOMIASIS

Bilharzia (schistosomiasis) is a disease caused by parasitic flat-worms, which choose the blood vessels of your bowel and bladder as the place they like to inhabit. Parasite larvae are released from freshwater snails. When infected water comes into contact with your skin, it's the chance of a lifetime for that part of the schisto parasite known as the cercaria. It pierces the skin (sometimes giving you 'swimmer's itch') and then travels via the lung to the bladder or bowel. Here, it starts reproducing, making loads of eggs which irritate your bowel or bladder

Bilharzia is common in sub-Saharan lakes

depending on which type of bilharzia you pick up. The freshwater lakes and rivers of sub-Saharan Africa are the main affected areas *(see map on page 10)*.

Schisto is common in travellers. Hundreds of gap-year travellers and people who just can't keep out of African lakes get it every year, and most don't know it. Many people brought up in sub-Saharan Africa, especially in rural areas, may have been infected since childhood.

Symptoms

One of three things can happen. In most cases, there are no symptoms at all. But it's still worth getting checked out if you could have been

exposed – you can be infected without knowing it. Unde-
tected bilharzia occasionally leads to more serious bladder,
liver or neurological problems months or years later.

Quite commonly, the infected person feels tired and
washed out, a full 10 years older for no apparent reason.
This could be the chronic form. Get a schisto blood test from
a high-quality lab, but keep in mind that the result only becomes reliable about 60 days or more after your last exposure. So this is often a useful test to have when you get home.

Wheezing, itchy skin, fever and muscle ache could mean
that the acute form of schisto, Katayama fever, is hitting you
(the timing is variable, but usually occurs 20 to 60 days after
exposure). See a doctor as soon as you can. Malaria and
other diseases, such as typhoid, also cause high fever, so have
yourself checked for these as well as bilharzia.

Prevention
Don't dive, snorkel, swim, wash, splash or fool around in
the rivers, lakes, ponds or neglected swimming pools of sub-
Saharan Africa. Lake Malawi is a particularly bad area. Also
avoid going near the overgrown margins of a lake or river;
the risk is usually less in the middle of a lake. You can also
become infected from washing or showering in water drawn

from an infected source which has not been allowed to stand for 48 hours. You can't get it from sea water.

A recent report from the London Hospital for Tropical Diseases suggests that applying 50 percent Deet to the whole body, excluding scalp and genitalia, after your evening wash on the day of exposure greatly reduces the chance of getting infected.

Treatment

If your test is positive, praziquantel tablets cure about 95 percent of infections. The usual treatment is a single dose of 40mg per kilogram of body weight. In some countries, including the UK, praziquantel can be hard to get hold of.

DENGUE FEVER

Dengue (pronounced 'dengee') fever is a nasty flu-like illness spread by Aedes mosquitoes. In Southeast Asia and parts of South America and the Caribbean, dengue fever is more common than malaria. The map on page 10 shows the main risk areas for this re-emerging disease.

The Aedes is a cousin of the Anopheles mosquito that causes malaria. A&A Ltd have carved out an empire for themselves by setting up a shift system. Aedes favours the morning and afternoon (especially the warm later afternoon), and Anopheles takes over for the evening and night.

So this means that you can catch dengue from day-biting mosquitoes.

Aedes also does well in cities – it has mastered the art of racing through its life cycle, so has little problem breeding in old tyres, air-

Once bitten, twice...

Try hard to avoid getting dengue fever more than once, because of the severity of subsequent bouts and the possibility of developing dengue haemorrhagic fever.

conditioner vents, the tops of bamboo poles, rusty old pipes – anywhere where water collects.

Along with many tropical diseases, dengue is making a comeback. It's common in travellers, and if you're making a short trip to or through a dengue zone, it often welcomes you back home, appearing a day or so after you get off the plane. The science behind that is its incubation period: 8 to 10 days. So it's possible to be bitten in Bangkok on Saturday, fly back home a week later, and feel awful by Monday.

Symptoms

Dengue fever is also known as breakbone fever because it feels as though your bones are breaking, especially the ones in your back. The muscles, joints and head all start hurting; you may develop a rash.

Dengue has another trick; just when you think you're getting better, it comes back again. In some cases, the disease makes people bleed into the skin, although that's rare in travellers. Second or subsequent bouts tend to be more severe

than the initial one. Also, if you've had dengue fever before, you may be at greater risk of getting dengue haemorrhagic fever – symptoms include bleeding into the skin and gums – which is much more dangerous.

Dengue usually reduces the blood cells known as platelets, and this helps lab technicians identify the problem. There's also a special blood test available in some countries, but it usually takes several days to give a result.

Prevention

Dengue can strike in cities, and it likes wet conditions

Dengue tends to be commoner in the wet season and often comes in epidemics, so when you hear from from the local media or tourist grapevine that dengue's in town, be sure to take some preventative steps. Cover up and use Deet, especially during the riskiest hours, the morning and afternoon. There's no vaccine.

Treatment

You don't want to mess with dengue. If you think you may have it, be sure to get checked out by a doctor. Dengue and malaria have similar symptoms, so if you think you may have dengue, ask for a malaria test as well.

• Realise there's no specific cure or treatment, just patience and rest, allowing yourself time to recover and seeking medical help if your symptoms get worse.

• Go to bed, take some painkillers (not containing aspirin), pray your friends haven't also caught it, and be patient.

• Sometimes it leaves an after-effect, making you feel depressed and listless for weeks – months if you're unlucky.

• If you become seriously ill or notice any bruising or bleeding, get urgent medical care.

Chikungunya fever

A dengue lookalike, also caused by a virus and spread by a mosquito, is making a comeback in South Asia and the islands of the Indian Ocean. It's called Chikungunya fever. It resembles dengue and can also cause painful joints, sometimes giving you a stooping walk. Treat it in the same way as dengue, but make sure you get good medical advice if you suspect you have it.

HEPATITIS

Hepatitis is an infection of the liver caused by one of several types of virus. It's the commonest cause of jaundice. You can pick up any of the four main types of hepatitis when travelling. It's helpful to think of them in pairs, A and E spread through the mouth and B and C spread more like HIV.

Hepatitis A, the commonest type, is spread by close contact with someone who is infected (or infectious without knowing it). The germs from the infectious faeces of one person contaminate the food or water used by another, or they get transferred on cups, utensils and towels. This means it commonly affects several members of the same household. Africa, Asia and Latin America are the main danger areas. Hepatitis E may be more common than is realised. It's similar to hepatitis A but is dangerous during pregnancy. Hepatitis B is spread largely through unprotected sex, or unclean needles. Hepatitis C is less common and is spread by infected blood transfusions, needles and body piercing.

Symptoms

Hepatitis starts with fever, chills, aching and nausea, so it can mimic malaria. Sometimes there's also pain over the liver. The urine goes darker, stools paler and your eyes look yellow. Nausea and weakness may persist for days or weeks. Hepatitis can make you feel very ill and low in spirits for several weeks, and recovery to full strength can take a long time. If you have suspicious symptoms, it is always worth seeing a doctor, having medical tests carried out and following specific advice.

Prevention

Hepatitis A can be prevented by a vaccine *(see page 28)* – the only reliable way of avoiding it. Good personal hygiene is important also; see the section on diarrhoea *(page 51)* for advice. Scrupulous hygiene will also protect against hepatitis E; there's no vaccine yet. Hepatitis B is easy to prevent through immunisation. To prevent hepatitis C, avoid blood transfusions and unsterilised needles and syringes; there's no vaccine.

Recovery and Follow-up

Resting until you feel better is the key to recovery. Sweet drinks are said to ease the nausea.

Liver function tests are available in many countries and help to monitor progress, but you normally know when you're recovering because you start to feel better. Some labs can carry out tests to see which of the four types of hepatitis you may have. In the case of B and C you will need careful follow-up, because further liver problems can develop later, and partial treatment is available. Some other diseases cause jaundice or give raised results in liver function tests, so always see a doctor rather than trying to diagnose yourself.

Typhoid can be picked up from contaminated water

TYPHOID

Typhoid (also known as enteric fever) is caused by Salmonella typhi, a brother in crime of the food-poisoning bug some of us have had from eating bad eggs or chicken at home. It's picked up from contaminated food and water. Sometimes a person is a carrier of typhoid germs without knowing it – bad news when it's a cook. Typhoid is found almost anywhere in the tropics or hot climates.

If you get a fever or become ill when travelling in developing countries, odds are that a local doctor (after excluding malaria) will think you've got typhoid. Often that's because the test that is normally used (the Widal) is very inaccurate, and if you've had your typhoid jab the test is often positive anyway. However, typhoid is common and serious. You can still get it, or one of its cousins such as paratyphoid, even if you've had your typhoid jab.

Symptoms

Typhoid symptoms include a high temperature, usually climbing gradually rather than going up and down as in malaria. A cough is common early, diarrhoea later, usually bodyache, and sometimes a faint rash. Often typhoid fever is hard to diagnose when symptoms first appear, and only later is it confirmed to be the cause. Sometimes typhoid just gives you a severe or persistent illness, with malaria tests negative.

Prevention

Make sure you're vaccinated before heading off to problem areas, but remember the vaccine is not 100 percent effective. Be very careful about what you eat and drink. See the section on diarrhoea *(page 51)* for Dos and Don'ts.

Treatment

It's the same advice as usual when you feel ill abroad. Seek out the best doctor in town, make sure you've not got malaria, and go along with any reasonable treatment you might be offered. The various antibiotics commonly used are ampicillin, Augmentin, cotrimoxazole (Septrin), chloramphenicol and ciprofloxacin. There is increasing drug resistance to typhoid, and in most areas it's probably best to opt for 'cipro'; you may have some in your diarrhoea kit. Treatment should be for 14 days, 500mg twice daily.

ALL CREATURES GREAT AND SMALL

Some animals constitute real health problems for travellers. Among the big bullies are dogs, already given a bad press under rabies *(see page 68)*. There's also a large choice of smaller creatures to be aware of. Some other little creatures are responsible for problems with travellers' skin – see the next chapter.

Bed Bugs

Avoiding these is hardly a genuine reason for staying in five-star hotels. However, bugs are common in budget hotels, and a line of angry, large, itchy bites is an increasingly common part of a travel experience. Fortunately bed bugs do not spread any serious illnesses.

Bed bugs come out at night, eat you for dinner, and cause you few problems apart from their graffiti and disturbing your sleep. They are oval, brown and wingless, about 5mm (¼in) long or less. Don't scratch the bites or they will itch for days. Apply calamine lotion and/or 1 percent hydrocortisone cream and take antihistamines (eg chlorphenamine – Piriton – 4mg tablets); keep in mind that antihistamines may make you drowsy.

Change hotels. If bed bugs have invaded your home or bedding, put all beds, bedding, sleeping bags etc. out into full sun for a day. This usually kills off the bugs.

One way to prevent bed-bug bites is to sleep under a tucked-in permethrin-impregnated mosquito net, having first checked

To remove ticks
Gently grasp the head end with blunt tweezers, push gently downwards to disengage the head, twisting gently from side to side; take care to squeeze as little as possible. After removal apply iodine or alcohol.

bed bugs are not hiding in the bed or bedding, and use a permethrin-impregnated undersheet. Leaving the light on also helps deter them.

Ticks

These very small, eight-legged creatures bury into your skin. The first sign of a tick bite is usually a bump or strange spot on your skin which gradually gets bigger. If you feel ill or develop a rash or fever after a tick bite, see a doctor at once. Ticks can cause typhus (in many parts of the world), Lyme disease in the USA and parts of Europe including the UK, and tick-borne encephalitis mainly in Central and Eastern Europe. Be extra cautious if travelling in the African savannah, monsoon Asia or the forests of Eastern Europe (see page 30).

Precautions

To prevent tick bites, apply Deet insect repellent to your skin, or soak your trousers or socks in permethrin. Tuck your trouser legs into thick socks and wear strong shoes or boots. If in a tick-rich zone check your own body and that of any companion before going to bed to make sure no ticks are attached in parts of your body you may not be aware of.

Intestinal Worms

No trip to the tropics would be complete if you didn't bring back a few slimy souvenirs. The most common to enter your gastrointestinal tract without permission are: pin, whip, round, hook and tape worms. Some show on stool tests, but most don't unless the worms have recently been reproducing in your dark interior.

Treatment
When you get home, or every six months if you linger in the tropics, take some mebendazole 100mg tablets, one tablet twice daily for three days; it zaps all worms except tapeworm. Alternatives are mebendazole 500mg or albendazole 400mg, just one of either. See a doctor if you pass any worm or worm fragments, ideally taking along a sample of your stool.

Leeches

Leeches are blood-sucking, worm-like creatures common in the forested areas of Asia, especially during the monsoon. They wait by a path and seek out your legs (or other parts depending on what you are doing). Leeches don't spread illnesses, and treatment is needed only if bites become infected.

Typical leech country

The dreaded scorpion

Precautions

• Wear stout boots and long trousers firmly tucked into socks – but the highest-IQ leeches may still get to you. Soak trousers and socks in permethrin to increase your protection.

• If leeches become attached, don't panic: they rarely cause problems unless you forcibly detach them, when they may leave their head parts behind, which can cause infection.

• Some experts recommend leaving leeches alone to fall off naturally. If this does not appeal, remove them by applying salt or alcohol, which usually causes them to writhe and fall off, but your skin may ooze blood for hours afterwards.

• If a leech attaches itself to an embarrassing part of you, let it finish its meal and detach itself naturally.

Scorpions

Stings by scorpion are usually painful, often severely so, but only sometimes dangerous. The main danger areas depends on the species, but you should take extra caution in Central and South America, North Africa, the Middle East, South Africa and South Asia. If you are likely to be exposed, check out the availability of antivenom locally and how it should be used.

Precautions

Wear shoes where scorpions are common, shine a torch into dark areas, and shake out shoes, trousers (especially the legs) and sleeping bags before using them. If setting up camp in an area where scorpions are present, first try to locate, then avoid or dig out scorpion tunnels.

Treatment

To treat scorpion bites, keep the affected area still if possible. Use the pain relief described below. See a doctor if the area is very swollen or painful, or you're feeling unwell.

Pain relief takes the form of a lignocaine 2 percent injection, or pethidine if very severe, or rubbing in EMLA cream (available on prescription in the UK) or taking another strong painkiller.

Snakes

Lethal snakebites are rare in travellers, but poisonous snakes are found throughout virtually the whole of the tropics, so the risk is real.

Precautions

Minimise your chances of being bitten by:

• Keeping completely still if you come across a snake. It will probably slink away unless you find it seeking your warmth and sharing your bed (very rare but then keep completely still until the snake leaves as the day warms up).

Uninvited guest

• If sleeping outside in areas where snakes are common, use a hammock or sleep at least 1m (3ft) off the ground under a mosquito net tightly tucked in.

• Use common sense in snake-infested areas; imagine where snakes might be and avoid putting your hand in holes, dense vegetation or on ledges that you can't see. Check beds, sleeping bags and footwear.

• Wear strong shoes and boots when walking in long grass or other areas where snakes are common. When out at night always use a strong torch.

• Remember that snakes sometimes come into houses, especially ground-floor bathrooms and kitchens.

• Avoid swimming in overgrown rivers and lakes or in mangroves. Sea snakes are found around the Asian coastline and tropical islands, down the coast of East Africa and around the Australian coast except in the south.

Symptoms

Don't panic if bitten. Many snakes fail to inject much venom when they bite. Even if they do, lethal effects usually take hours to develop, although there are exceptions. Look for the following symptoms, which depend on the type of snake.

• Pain, blistering and swelling near the bite and up the limb (from any poisonous snake).

• Generalised bleeding, for example noticed from gums and nose (especially from vipers and rattlesnakes).

• Weakness and paralysis of muscles, often first shown by drooping eyelids, then trouble swallowing or breathing (especially from sea snakes, cobras, kraits and mambas).

Treatment

• Keep the affected body part (usually the leg or arm) as still as possible and below the level of the heart.

• If easy to do, apply a firm bandage to the arm or leg and splint if possible, or put the arm in sling.

• Give maximum reassurance to the victim.

• To kill the pain, use paracetamol (1,000mg), codeine (60mg) or dihydrocodeine (30mg), but not aspirin.

• Get to the nearest, best medical facility as quickly as you possibly can.

• If antivenom is used, make sure adrenalin (epinephrine) is available to deal with any allergic reaction, and treatment is administered by someone medically qualified. The same dose of antivenom is used for children as for adults.

• If possible, take the snake with you in a container (only if dead) to the doctor or hospital for identification. This may help to determine treatment. Otherwise, carefully note the snake's appearance.

• Contrary to what you may have learnt from movies, don't suck, incise or squeeze the bite and don't apply a tourniquet on the limb above the bite.

Antivenom supply

If you're a zoologist or anyone else likely to be exposed to snakes, especially in remote areas, consider taking along some antivenom from a regional supply centre. It can be difficult to get hold of, however.

Crocodiles

Every year travellers and many more local residents become a meal for crocs. Get expert local knowledge before venturing into a seductive gleam of water, or walking too near to river banks or lakesides. East Africa, Borneo, Florida and northern Australia regularly supply backpacker meals for rogue reptiles.

Other Aquatic Dangers

Many dangerous aquatic animals are most common in the Indo-Pacific region. They include:

• Box jellyfish, especially off the coasts of Australia and the Philippines. These potentially deadly creatures are present at certain times of year, for example during the wet season in northern Australia. Apply vinegar and get antivenom urgently. For more information, see <www.aims.gov.au>.

Don't get between a hippo and the water!

• Spiny fish that puncture the skin. Immerse in hot water, extract spine and in the case of stonefish get antivenom.

Symptoms of envenoming are one or some of the following: sudden pain, diarrhoea, vomiting, sweating, difficulty breathing.

• Jellyfish and their relatives may leave linear rashes. Use vinegar, steroid cream or tablets, and seek medical care.
• Sea urchins can detach bits of themselves, usually into your feet. Remove spines carefully after softening the skin with 2 percent salicylic acid ointment.
• Coral cuts. Remove all pieces methodically, otherwise healing can take a long time. Get medical advice.

Precautions
• Get local advice about the dangers of swimming in unfamiliar locations.
• Avoid getting close to any venomous creature when bathing or wading, and avoid areas known to be used by sharks and other predators. This is especially important if menstruating or if you have a bleeding wound.
• Wear a lycra stinger suit if swimming or diving in unsafe waters. These suits protect against venomous sea creatures and help to prevent injuries from coral.
• Avoid coral cuts by taking great care on coral reefs.

BODY PROBLEMS

Skin

If you normally live in a temperate climate, your skin may not thrive in the tropics. Sweat, bugs, rubbing and being tired all make the skin more likely to get boils, fungal infections and other blobs and blotches. And then there are bites. So check your skin often, treat infections early, avoid getting sunburnt, use insect repellents, eat a healthy diet and wash daily with soap and water. See a doctor if things get serious.

Some common skin problems and their treatment are given below. If your symptoms are not here, see a local doctor, but if you and they remain puzzled take a digital photo and send it to a doctor or skin specialist you may know at home.

Athlete's Foot

Athlete's foot is a common condition which gives you itching between the toes, especially the smaller ones. Prevent it by wearing open shoes, or a clean pair of cotton socks each day. If symptoms start, apply a fungicidal power, such as zinc undecanoate or a product containing it, between your toes each night. Clotrimazole cream is also effective.

Cellulitis

Cellulitis is caused by a bacterial infection, and is common in hot and humid climates. It shows itself as a hot, red patch, spreading up your leg, or less commonly on other parts of the body. Rest, and if it is your leg that is affected keep it elevated and immobile. Quickly obtain flucloxacillin 500mg and take four times daily, and/or amoxicillin 500mg three times daily, both for a week. Use these antibiotics together if seriously affected, ill or feverish. If you're allergic to penicillin, use erythromycin 500mg every six hours. See a doctor.

> **Jigger flea eggs**
>
> Pea-size swelling on the foot or near the toes? If you are in Africa or South America, it could be the eggs of a jigger flea. Get an expert to remove the eggs with a sterile needle, and apply an antiseptic cream, or alcohol, to prevent infection. Prevent further problems by wearing enclosed shoes, not sandals or flip-flops.

Eczema

Eczema is an inflammation of the skin, which becomes dry, hot and itchy. You may recognise it from having had eczema in the past. Although eczema some-times improves when travelling in warm climates, it's not always pos-sible to predict this, and sometimes it becomes infected more easily. Use mild hydrocortisone, plus an-tibiotics by mouth if yellow or green pus is on the surface. Get this checked out. It can mimic a fungus.

Fungal Infection (Ringworm)

Is your rash itchy and round with spreading edge? If so, it's probably a fungus. Rub in an antifungal cream, con-tinuing for 10 days after it seems to have cleared up. Use Daktarin cream (miconazole) or Can-esten cream (clotrimazole).

Impetigo

Impetigo is a bacterial skin infection, commonly found on the face or neck. The symptoms are red, inflamed warm skin that oozes a honey-coloured fluid. Similar treat-ment to cellulitis *(see page 108)*, plus antibiotic or antisep-tic cream. It's extremely infectious, so keep away from others, have your own towel, and wash frequently.

Lice

Lice are very small creatures that infest the body's hair. Their eggs, called nits, show up as dandruff-like objects firmly at-tached to hair shafts usually in the scalp, sometimes in the pubic hair. Pubic lice often cause itching. Lice are common world-wide, especially among children or in poor living conditions.

Good personal hygiene helps to prevent lice infestation, as does regular wet combing. There are many preparations available, but lice are often resistant. Get local advice, otherwise try 1 percent malathion or lindane shampoo, or permethrin 1 percent cream rinse, repeating each after seven days. Read the manufacturer's instructions. Pubic lice can be treated in a similar way, but apply the preparation to the whole body, excluding the scalp but including the beard. Your partner should be treated too. Clothes should be washed in hot water. See <www.nits.net>.

Melanoma

Melanoma, the most dangerous form of skin cancer, is caused by prolonged exposure to the sun. If you have a mole or dark

Prolonged exposure to the sun is not a good idea

spot which is getting bigger, darker, less regular, or itches, bleeds or oozes, get it seen at once. It probably won't turn out to be melanoma, but it's very important to have a good doctor confirm that. This also applies to any active-looking skin problem, especially on skin that has had a lot of sun exposure in the past.

Cutaneous Larva Migrans or CLM

A squiggly red line under the skin of the feet or bottom probably indicates cutaneous larva migrans (CLM), also known as sandworm. This is picked up from walking or sitting (especially above the high tide line) on a dirty beach which dogs use as their toilet. Get hold of albendazole 400mg tablets and take two daily for five days.

Scabies

If you develop spots that itch mainly at night, unless they are bites, you most likely have scabies, especially if the spots are near the genitals, round your waist, or on wrists and hands. Your friends or partner may also have this. Scabies, caused by the tiny Sarcoptes mite which burrows under your skin, is common worldwide, but especially in crowded conditions and among budget travellers.

Use 5 percent permethrin cream or 0.5 percent malathion over the whole body up to the neckline, leave for at least 12 hours, then wash off. Alternatively, use benzyl benzoate the same way; be careful, as it can sting mucous membranes. Also effective are Ivermectin tablets (Mectizan) at a dose of 0.2mg per kilogram of body weight; repeat after 10 days. Ivermectin can also be used for lice *(see pages 109–10)*. Itching can persist for weeks after treatment. It is ideal for everyone who has been in close contact with the infected person, especially those sharing beds, sheets or towels, to be treated in the same way. Put fabrics, clothes and sheets which may have been in touch with your skin in full sun, or wash in very hot water.

Spots and Boils

These are common when you are hot, tired or stressed. For those working abroad it often means it's time for a good holiday. Take frequent showers and use an antiseptic soap. The staph bugs that cause boils also live in the nostrils, so put antibiotic or antiseptic cream into the lower nostril every night; Naseptin is a good brand. Don't scratch bites. Work less hard, sleep more and take a holiday, especially if boils keep coming. Then also take flucloxacillin 500mg every six hours (that is, four times a day) for seven days as soon as another one raises its ugly head (if allergic to penicillin, use erythromycin instead – same dose, same frequency).

Ears

An infected ear canal is a common and painful condition in travellers, more common and severe when you're tired and do a lot of swimming, especially in unclean water. Two things make it worse, and you can do something about each:

• Having wax in your ear or a recent infection in your ear canal. See your doctor or practice nurse and get this seen to before going abroad: wax removed, infection treated.

Skin Deep: the Tumbu Larva

A boil that persists, is very painful, seems to move, and has two black dots appearing at the surface is probably a Tumbu fly larva or close cousin, found in East and Central Africa and parts of Latin America. Apply Vaseline or oil at night to suffocate the larva and ask a health worker or non-squeamish friend to press out the maggot the following day. Prevent this from happening again by drying underwear and shirts on a clothes line in full sun, or inside the house, then hot-ironing to kill any eggs the Tumbu fly may have laid on your clothes.

• Swimming without ensuring that you drain all the water from your ear immediately afterwards. Tilt your head, gently apply a towel end to the outer part of your ear, and drain all the water.

Treatment

See a doctor, or get hold of some ear drops such as Gentisone HC, an antibiotic and steroid combination.

If very painful, or there's pus discharging from your ear, or you have a fever, also take antibiotics by mouth, for example amoxicillin 500mg capsules three times a day for a week or, if allergic to penicillin, erythromycin 500mg four times a day for a week. These antibiotics will usually help a middle-ear infection or infected eardrum to settle down too.

Pressure Problems

Painful ears on a flight are usually due to pressure changes. Suck a sweet, and if you know from the past this may be a problem, consider taking one ibuprofen 400mg tablet with one decongestant tablet, for example pseudoephedrine 60mg, about an hour before the flight or an hour before descent.

Eyes

Eye problems should never be ignored, especially in the tropics, where infection gets going fast. See a doctor early if your eyes start causing serious grief. If you wear contacts, talk to your contact lens practitioner before you go. Take all the contact lens supplies you need, as well as two spare pairs of glasses. If you have glaucoma or there is a family history of it, get your eye pressures measured.

Conjunctivitis

Conjunctivitis is common in hot and humid climates, especially if you're tempted to touch or rub your eyes. Your eyes

will probably be red, sore, gritty, blurry and sticky in the morning. Get hold of chloramphenicol eye drops or other antibiotic eye drops and use every two hours. Make sure the drops do not also contain a steroid, unless prescribed by a doctor skilled or experienced in treating eye conditions. Also see an ophthalmologist if you wear contact lenses or if there is no rapid improvement in your symptoms. And, of course, remove your contacts if you wear them.

Other Eye Problems

Other eye problems can also occur, the commonest being styes. If you have one, apply a warm compress, take a painkiller and don't be tempted to squeeze it. If the stye doesn't quickly settle down, treat with antibiotics as described above for ear problems *(see page 112)*.

Itchy, dry eyes have various causes. It's better to seek health advice, but first try using artificial tears such as Hypotears. If your eyes go yellow, you may have jaundice *(see page 95)*.

(see page 112)
(see page 95)

Eye protection

Protect your eyes from ultraviolet light by using sunglasses in bright sun, remembering that in some cultures wearing these does not help to build trust, especially for males. Use snow goggles above the snowline or in polar conditions.

FLU AND AVIAN (BIRD) FLU

Influenza

Flu is found worldwide and occurs in epidemics mainly in the winter months. It's common among travellers, especially in crowded environments such as cruise ships. The currently available flu vaccine for the hemisphere you are travelling to will usually prevent it *(see page 29)*. If you are over 65 or have a significant health problem including a tendency to chest infections, you should have the vaccine before travelling. Your own country will probably have guidelines for you to follow.

Flu is spread by droplet infection; in other words if you cough or sneeze, people breathe in your germs. But it's also spread by dirty hands, so shaking hands and hot-desking with computers can also spread it. Regular hand-washing is one of the most useful things travellers can do to avoid infections.

Avian (Bird) Flu

Avian (bird) flu occurs mainly in birds, but in recent years a number of human infections have been reported. At the time of writing these have occurred in only a few countries, mainly in Southeast Asia. The risk to travellers is low.

Symptoms

Although the symptoms are not yet fully defined, most people infected develop flu-like symptoms after 10 days, become rapidly ill and develop a cough and fever (above 38°C/ 100°F). Children appear to be the most easily infected.

Prevention

During travel to an infected area, avoid contact with living or dead poultry or wild birds. Don't visit or stay with families keeping domestic poultry. Avoid contact with surfaces contaminated with animal faeces or secretions, and wash

Wild birds – a very low risk to travellers

your hands frequently. Don't eat raw or undercooked poultry or poultry products, including eggs.

If You Become Unwell
If you start to feel ill, it's highly unlikely that avian flu is the cause. If you develop a fever, cough, sore throat or difficulty breathing, consult a doctor and say if you've had direct contact with poultry.

Treatment
At the time of writing there's no vaccine to protect against avian flu. The effectiveness of antiviral drugs before or during a pandemic has not been reliably tested.

The antiviral drug oseltemavir (Tamiflu) should be started, under medical supervision as soon as possible, ideally within 48 hours of any symptoms, but may be worth giving at any stage in the illness. The recommended dose is 150mg daily.

IF YOU HAVE A FEVER

Make sure that what you're experiencing is a genuine fever, because you can be shivering or sweating with a normal body temperature. Our normal temperature can vary quite a bit, but it should be at or below 37°C (98.6°F). Most fevers disappear on their own, no cause is found and they are assumed to be the result of a virus. But when travelling, especially in the tropics, take fever more seriously, especially if it persists, recurs or reaches above 38°C (100°F). In malarious areas, assume that a fever is malaria until proved otherwise. For fever in children also read the section on pages 123–8.

If you have a fever, see a doctor. In this section there's a checklist of possible causes, but this is not meant to worry you, and it's not meant to be a substitute for asking a doctor to try to find the cause and give you the right treatment.

Causes of Fever in the Tropics

Below are some of the tropical diseases that cause fever. Many of them are extemely rare among travellers.

- Amoebic dysentery or abscess *(see pages 57–8)*.
- Bacillary (bacterial) dysentery *(see pages 58–9)*.

Non-Tropical Causes of Fever

Non-tropical causes of fever include measles, chickenpox, rubella, mumps, glandular fever and cytomegalovirus, gastroenteritis, diverticulitis (especially in the older traveller), appendicitis, pelvic tract infections, renal tract infections including cystitis and pyelonephritis (kidney infection), tonsillitis, ear and sinus infections, bronchitis, pneumonia, flu and related viruses, skin infections such as cellulitis, boils and abscesses. Other causes of fever are blood poisoning, tooth infections and rare cancers.

- Bilharzia or schistotosomiasis *(see page 90).*
- Brucellosis from infected milk – mainly Africa and West Asia.
- Chagas disease, the South American form of sleeping sickness, caused by the bite of an 'assassin bug' in mud houses.
- Chikungunya fever *(see page 95).*
- Dengue fever *(see pages 92–5).*
- Ebola and other viral haemorrhagic fevers – very rare and localised – severe fever, muscle ache, sore throat and rash.
- Heatstroke *(see page 81).*
- Hepatitis A, B, C or E, usually with yellow eyes *(see page 95).*
- HIV infection *(see page 75).*
- Japanese encephalitis with severe headache – South and Southeast Asia only.
- Lassa fever, severely ill with ulcerated sore throat and muscle pains – rural areas of West Africa: an emergency.
- Legionnaire's disease, giving severe pneumonia.
- Leptospirosis, giving headache, severe muscle pain and jaundice, usually from dirty water in irrigation canals and ponds.
- Malaria *(see page 61).*
- Meningitis with severe headache, stiff neck and non-blanching rash in the most serious form – no time to lose.
- STIs – some give fever *(see page 78).*
- Sleeping sickness with headache, swollen glands, tiredness caused by tsetse fly bite, usually when on safari in East and Central Africa; rare in travellers.
- Tick-bite fever in Africa – sometimes with a rash and swollen glands, but often mimicking malaria.
- Tuberculosis with evening or night fever, cough and loss of weight, usually in longer-term travellers, health workers or those in close contact with TB patients.
- Typhoid and paratyphoid fevers *(see page 97).*
- Typhus fever – usually affecting trekkers in Africa and Asia, often with a rash, swollen glands and muscle ache.
- West Nile fever – worldwide, but mainly North America.

It's important to keep work and relaxation in balance

STRESS

This section is mainly for those going on longer trips or living or working abroad. But anyone can benefit from reading it.

Coping with Stress

If you're away for an extended period, you're likely to experience some stressful situations. If you're stress-prone, here are some coping strategies.

• Most of us need some personal space, some much more than others. Try to find a 'cave' you can retreat into, whether it's a book, a CD, a video or DVD, a favourite place, a game of squash, meditation or prayer.
• Be aware of the four phases of culture shock that you'll probably go through *(see pages 121–2)*.
• Keep life in balance. Don't become a workaholic.

• Know yourself and how you're likely to respond to different situations. This can help you to avoid situations you may not handle well, and plan your life in a way that works for you.

• Learn to laugh at situations and at yourself.

• Give yourself permission to be normal: most people from time to time feel like yelling, crying or jumping on the next plane home. If you can see this as a normal part of adapting and realise it's no big deal, that in itself can relieve stress.

• Keep a journal or diary and record the bad feelings and the down times as well as the good.

• Manage relationship problems. These are often the biggest source of stress on a holiday or posting abroad. When travelling with a friend or in a group, share your expectations and ideas before you go, so that you all 'own' the plans. Agree that you will be open with each other if you feel the trip is not working out. Realise together that you'll all have your off days.

• Keep in touch with friends by texting, emails or phone.

• Take regular exercise – zap the stress by upping the heartbeat.

• Realise one person's stress is another person's stimulus. For example, an extra trip, party or event, may be just what your friend needs, but is the last straw for you.

• Make sure you get enough sleep and eat a healthy diet.

When It All Gets Too Much

For those on missions or assignments abroad, if something really needs sorting out, such as a relationship or problem in your placement, be proactive and talk to someone about it. Don't let the resentment, uncertainty or even depression set in. If everything seems to be getting on top of you, tell a friend, your employer or your host: that's not being weak, it's being sensible. Don't relieve your stress by doing crazy things now that might create problems later, such as binge drinking, doing drugs, or having inappropriate or unprotected sex.

CULTURE SHOCK

This section is mainly for people who are living, working or travelling abroad for some time.

Culture shock is the stress and unhappiness felt by people who live in cultures that are very different from their own. When we live abroad for a while we're almost bound to have our ups and downs. Real travel means a mixture of brilliant days and times you never want to think about again. So when you feel like jumping on the next plane or you definitely can't stand the heat, the smell, or your roommate one more day, just remember

Foreign climes can sometimes seem overwhelming

– that sort of thing is normal. It's very hard to predict culture shock. Most of us get it – a few of us don't.

Adjustment Phases

Quite apart from good days and bad, many of us go through a particular cycle, however long we're abroad. Psychologists talk about four phases: elation, depression, recovery and acculturation.

Elation. It's brilliant. Great sights, sounds, experiences. Freedom, fun, cool cities, great safaris, friendly locals.

Depression. It's awful. What! I wrote home and said how

Homesickness soon fades

great it was? Hard beds, floppy beds, noise all night, hot, sweaty, exhausted, so much dirt and hassle. Mum I'm missing you, and Jack, Ali, Pablo and Flopsy the dog.

Recovery. It's OK. I'm getting used to the hassles. I'm making some good friends. I was really homesick over Christmas/Eid/my birthday, but I survived and we had fun. On the whole I'm enjoying it.

Acculturation. It's great here. I just don't want to go home. I love the people – they are so real, so friendly. Anyway, I think I chose the wrong course to do at college, so I think I'll tell Dad I'm going to stay out here. All those boring things my friends at home were always talking about – I bet they still are. It's so crowded and cold and grey back home. Anyway I've met this wonderful person...

How to Make Things Easier

To help adapt to your new surroundings and reduce culture shock, follow the suggestions for combating stress (see page 119). Some more advice is given below. You can read about reverse culture shock on pages 138–40.

• Develop self-awareness. Understand yourself and the phases in the diagram.
• Learn about the place you're going to; pick up some language skills; get clued-up ahead of time.
• Avoid diarrhoea (see page 51) and keep healthy!

SPECIAL ADVICE

TRAVELLING WITH CHILDREN

This section is aimed at parents taking children with them, especially if travelling independently or for a longer period. See also the index for other related topics.

Travelling with children can be a great delight or a major hassle, and is commonly a mixture of both. There are two secrets that help to make travelling with kids a great experience. The first is being very well prepared before you go, and the second is having the confidence that you have thought of almost everything. Then you can relax and avoid getting too stressed when the first challenge comes.

Most of us taking children abroad will be mainly concerned with their happiness, safety and health. These three overlap, of course, so although this section is mainly about health, it covers some of the other areas, too.

The only way to travel

Before You Go

Understand your children. Do they like change and adventure and the unfamiliar, or does this tend to worry or scare them? Choose a holiday or trip that's likely to be mainly within their comfort zone, or at least not largely outside of it. Choose a country, a place to stay, an itinerary or an activity that's likely to work for the children. Happy kids usually mean happy adults – so the whole venture needs to be primarily planned for the children. Will the climate suit them, the sleeping arrangements work, the plans for the day be suitable? And don't forget the local culture, transport and the length of the flight.

Help them to understand as much as they can about where you're going and what to expect. Talking about the trip or holiday helps children to feel excited rather than anxious. But don't overdo this, so that when children fail to see elephants or camels, or the surfing and water-skiing are not as great as you expected, they don't get seriously disappointed.

Plenty to look forward to

Unless this is a simple package holiday, have a travel health consultation with your usual doctor, nurse or other health worker who is well informed about travel health. This is what you must have in place for children before travel:

• Essential immunisations, both the normal childhood jabs and any needed especially for the trip.
• Information about how to

prevent and treat the most likely problems that may affect them, such as sunburn, prickly heat, diarrhoea and, if relevant, malaria.

• Health supplies *(see page 32)*, which need to include the particular things children need, such as special preparations of essential medicines, the right type of mosquito net and the right strength of insect repellent and suncream.

• Knowing about health care abroad: what to do and who to see if your children or any other members of the group get ill in the country you are going to.

• Travel health insurance that covers the children.

The Flight

• Check ahead with the airline or tour operator about seats and in-flight arrangements for children. Book seats that are convenient, for example bulkhead seats which give you more space, or others with easy access to aisles and toilets.

• On a long flight, have a good selection of toys that can be brought out at appropriate moments.

• Help children to understand how to access music, films etc. – they, of course, may help you. Using in-flight entertainment keeps many children happy for hours.

• Make sure your children get enough to drink – they can get very thirsty on planes, a common cause of irritability.

• If the flight is bumpy or things happen which scare your children, explain what's happening so they understand that it's just part of what normally happens during flying.

• If your children have previously had ear pain when flying, give them some paracetamol syrup an hour before the flight. Sucking sweets, which leads to frequent swallowing, can help to make the ears less painful.

• Only use something to sedate your children on planes if it's really necessary or the flight is very long. Promethazine (Phenergan) is commonly used, but try it at home first, because occasionally it stimulates children rather than helping them to go to sleep.

At Your Destination

• Make sure your children don't get separated from you, all too easy when adults are distracted and the children are excited by new sights and sounds.
• Persuade your children not to touch or play with any animals, especially dogs.
• Take extra care crossing roads.
• Protect your children from sunburn *(see page 79)*.
• If you're in a malarious area, be very careful not to miss the malaria pills and try to avoid insect bites.
• Assess any hazards in your accommodation, the transport you use (where possible), and daily activities.

Illness Abroad: What to Do

Most illnesses that children get abroad are not serious and are not travel-related: they are just as likely to happen at home. But you need to be aware of serious illnesses that are present locally, such as malaria and dengue fever, and make sure you know whom to see and where to go if your children become ill.

Finally – though this is easier said than done – the more relaxed parents are, the more the children will pick up the good vibes and enjoy themselves.

An Action Plan

• Assess how ill the child is. An important part of this is taking the temperature – so make sure you have a thermometer and use it. If the temperature is above 38°C (100°F) you need to take the illness seriously. See a doctor if possible, especially if malaria is a possibility.
• Be alert for any unusual symptoms, such as a severe

headache, vomiting or a rash. If the child has any of these, see a doctor quickly, just in case it's meningitis.

• To help give you an idea of what the problem could be, see Common Health Problems *(below)* and also the list on pages 8–9. Remember that the commonest illnesses children get in most parts of the world are short-lived viral infections.

• If your child doesn't recover within two or three days, if the temperature remains above about 38°C (100°F), there is repeated vomiting, unusual symptoms develop, there is excessive drowsiness, severe headaches or the illness gets worse, you must see a well-informed doctor, preferably one who's used to seeing children (a paediatrician or good general physician).

Common Health Problems

• Accidents, especially road crashes but also dangers from beaches, pools, and at your accommodation *(see page 71)*.

• Croup is a scary noise in the throat when a child breathes in, and is especially worrying in children between 18 months and three years. Get immediate medical help.

Sleep Problems

You'll be very lucky if your children sleep right through the night from the word go. Children need to get used to their new home or environment. They will probably be excited, and may be puzzled or even scared by unusual sights or sounds, or by people and the way they speak or dress. Insisting on a normal bedtime can be counterproductive, especially to start with. It's a matter of spending some fun and relaxing time with the children, explaining anything that might be worrying them and making sure their sleeping arrangements are comfortable and reassuring. Sometimes it's better for younger children to sleep in the same room as you, even if you may not do this at home. Promethazine syrup *(see page 125)* may be used as a last resort.

• A breathing rate of 50 breaths or more per minute often means pneumonia, especially if there is in-drawing of the ribs. See a doctor and start antibiotics immediately.

• Get a cough that persists for more than three weeks checked.

• See a doctor quickly about wheezing, especially if it interferes with a child's normal activities or starts for the first time.

• Fever – if 38°C (100°F) or over. As well as seeing a doctor, try to bring the fever down, through undressing, sponging with tepid water and giving paracetamol syrup. If malaria is a possibility, see a doctor immediately.

• Headache, especially with stiff neck and/or vomiting. This could be meningitis – rare, but always serious.

• Skin problems. Clean cuts well, remove any dirt or foreign body, apply antiseptic cream and keep the injury covered with a light, non-adherent dressing to prevent further damage or dirt getting into the injury.

• Boils are common *(see page 112)*, especially if you stay for some time in hot climates.

• Foot injuries. On many holidays, children, and adults too, may swap shoes for flip-flops or go barefoot. This makes it much easier to injure feet, so wearing shoes outside the house or hotel room is a sensible thing to do.

• 'Creatures'. Discourage your children from touching or playing with unfamiliar dogs. Quite apart from the risk of rabies in some countries, you don't want to risk a bite or an unexpected growl, which scares your children. If you are living in an area where there are snakes or scorpions read pages 102–5.

WOMEN TRAVELLERS

Many health problems of relevance to women are mentioned elsewhere in the book, so this section concentrates on three topics: gynaecological problems, contraception and personal safety. There is a separate section on pregnancy on pages 133–6.

Gynae Problems

If you have any female health problems before travelling, it's worth getting these checked out prior to the big trip. Gynaecological problems can be doubly worrying abroad: first, any unfamiliar symptoms are worrying in themselves, and second, finding a good and ethical doctor in some countries can be difficult. Many women understandably want to see a doctor familiar with their own culture.

Period Problems

• **Light or absent periods.** It's very common for your cycle to change, especially when travelling for any length of time such as doing a round-the-world trip, a gap year or any adventure travel. Often periods stop altogether, sometimes for several months. Apart from making quite sure you're not pregnant, it's not usually anything to worry about unless you are unwell or have lost a lot of weight, either for no obvious reason or deliberately.

• **Heavy or irregular periods.** There are, of course, many causes for this, and only a few are serious. But if these symptoms persist beyond one or two cycles, it's worth getting checked out, especially if you have any prolonged or heavy bleeding, as this can lead to anaemia.

• **Preventing periods when travelling.** This is what most women will opt to do unless it's a long trip or you are living abroad. The simplest way is to take any contraceptive pill you are on continuously (but not biphasic or triphasic ones), ignoring the usual seven-day pill-free interval or the

Periods

Tampons are not easily available in many countries. Check with someone who knows the area you're going to and if in doubt take enough with you. Visiting some temples and especially mosques when having a period can be highly offensive if anyone finds out. And remember that certain sea animals such as sharks can be attracted by blood, as can land animals for example when on walking safaris, or when jogging.

seven days with an inactive ingredient. Some experts suggest it's not a good idea to do this for more than two or three cycles. If you are not on the pill and don't want to start using it, you can delay your period by taking norethisterone 5mg three times daily, starting three days before your expected period. Usually your period will come again two or three days after stopping. This hormone-based treatment in many countries has to be prescribed by a doctor.

It's probably worth trialling this before travelling to make sure it suits you.

• **Vaginal discharge.** This is common when travelling. Probably the commonest cause of abnormal discharge is candida or thrush, which usually involves a white itchy discharge. Being in a hot and humid climate, or on the pill, or taking doxycycline as an antimalarial can make this more likely. The simplest way of dealing with it is to use a single-dose clotrimazole (Canesten) 500mg pessary at night or to take a single fluconazole (Diflucan) 150mg tablet (not if pregnant). Read the patient information leaflet carefully.

There are, of course, other causes of an abnormal discharge, some caused by sexually transmitted infections. The commonest of these are trichomonas, chlamydia and gonorrhoea. It is essential to get any persisting discharge that's not normal for you carefully checked out during or after any overseas travel.

Sex and Contraception

HIV and other sexually transmitted diseases (STIs) are easily preventable *(see page 75)*. Using condoms carefully and reliably is the single most important way of avoiding an STI.

Which type of contraception to use is a highly personal choice, but if you're going abroad for a few months, consider an injectable contraceptive, an intra-uterine device (IUD) or a Mirena (a type of IUD). Otherwise the contraceptive pill is the most widely used method of birth control and the most reliable if you don't miss doses. For emergency contraception, take two tablets of levonorgestrel 0.75mg two hours apart.

Using the Contraceptive Pill Abroad

Holiday romance

• Take ample supplies of the pill with you, including the box or formulation (carry it separately, in case of loss or theft), so you know what type to get locally or to re-order from home.

• Crossing time zones. Check the instructions with the pill. You should not usually go longer than 27 hours between pills, and for the 'minipill' not more than 24 hours.

• If you forget a pill or have a bout of diarrhoea or vomiting, use additional contraception and follow the instructions on the leaflet.

• Types of pill: the combined oral contraceptive pill is

usually the best to use, rather than biphasic, triphasic or progesterone-only pills.

• Hot climates. The pill usually remains effective until its expiry date, but store it in as cool a place as you can.

Personal Safety

Quite apart from common-sense precautions that both men and women should take when in unfamiliar places, there are a few simple rules to prevent a lot of hassle for women, especially those who are travelling alone, off the beaten track or in places where tourists arouse interest.

• Dress modestly and avoid wearing tight or skimpy clothing, except in resorts and areas where the local people are very familiar with tourists and it is known to be safe. Dressing modestly is especially important in Islamic countries.

Travelling can be one of life's most rewarding experiences

• If you receive unwanted attention it may help to refer to your 'husband' or 'boyfriend'; you may even want to have a photo or wedding ring handy.

• Avoid eye-to-eye contact with men in countries where this is seen as a come-on. Dark glasses can be helpful.

• Consider taking a self-defence course before travelling independently. If attacked, be prepared to deliver a crippling blow if all else fails!

• Obtain first-hand advice about safe and unsafe areas in cities you are not familiar with.

• For casual sexual encounters, be bold in showing caution or negotiating condom use.

• Know emergency phone numbers and how to contact your embassy.

PREGNANCY

Large numbers of pregnant women travel worldwide, and few run into significant problems directly related to travel. But you still need to be very well informed about possible risks and what to do if a problem occurs. It's worth remembering that many pregnancy-related problems are unpredictable.

It's helpful to think about pregnancy under three headings: the safety of flying, the safety of visiting or living in a developing country, and the safety of giving birth overseas.

Flying and Other Forms of Travel

Most international airlines allow you to fly up to 35 weeks into your pregnancy, but check with your airline. Travelling during a normal trouble-free pregnancy causes only a few additional risks: the slightly greater danger that you might have an accident or illness, and the worry and inconvenience of being away from home and familiar medical facilities. Here are some travel tips during pregnancy:

• The safest time is generally between 18 and 26 weeks (low risk of miscarriage or premature labour).

• Air flight is safe – differences in cabin pressure and oxygen concentration do not harm a healthy mother or foetus.

• The seat belt in the plane (or any other vehicle) should be worn so the lap belt goes 'under the bump'.

• There is a slightly greater risk of developing deep vein thrombosis *(see page 42)*, especially for flights over five hours. Wear firmly fitting below-knee stockings. Low-dose aspirin at 75mg daily is considered safe in pregnancy, but has not been proved to reduce the risk of a DVT.

• Your feet may swell up more, especially in later pregnancy.

• Indigestion and flatulence can sometimes be more of a nuisance: avoid fizzy drinks.

• Airport security checks do not pose any radiation risks.

• Only have immunisations that are essential. Avoid live vaccines (check with your health adviser which ones these are) and the typhoid vaccine, as occasionally this can cause a fever.

When to Get Medical Advice

Some pregnant women should seek medical advice before travelling. See a doctor if you have:

• A pre-existing health problem which might add to the risk or discomfort of pregnancy during travel, such as a heart problem, diabetes, chronic back pain or a previous DVT.

• Problems in a previous pregnancy such as miscarriage, ectopic pregnancy or premature labour.

• Problems in your present pregnancy, such as a threatened miscarriage, vaginal bleeding, twins or an abnormal scan.

Pregnancy in Developing Countries

The safety of living or travelling in a developing country depends on how long you will be there, your stage of pregnancy, and how good and how near medical facilities are.

Here are some dangers to watch out for:

• **Malaria.** If you're going to a malarious area, especially where falciparum malaria is common, ask yourself if the trip is really necessary. If it is, take your antimalarial tablets, avoid being bitten and report any fever at once (*see page 61*).

• **Dangers from certain foods.** Follow the guidelines on pages 51–3 with extra care. Avoid soft cheeses and pâté because of the risk of Listeria.

• **Unnecessary medicines.** In many countries doctors prescribe a range of medicines if you become ill, and many are not needed at all. Only use medicines that are essential, and after you have checked in the patient information leaflet that they are safe to take during pregnancy.

• **Access to good health care.** Obviously this will vary enormously, but it's worth knowing which doctor you would see if a problem arises, so make enquiries if you're staying for any length of time.

Giving Birth Overseas

Most travellers will be planning to come home to have their baby, or at least to plan to have the delivery in a country or city with a high standard of medical care. If you plan to have your baby in a developing country make sure of the following:

Breastfeeding

Travel and breastfeeding go together very well. But in hot climates mothers will need to drink lots of extra fluid to keep up milk flow. If you use formula, take extra care to sterilise bottles, teats, etc. Avoid all but the most important immunisations. Make sure you take your antimalarial tablets if you need to, but discuss which medication to use with your doctor. Make sure any medicine you are given is safe to take when breastfeeding.

• There's a good-quality maternity unit with a doctor always on 24-hour call, able to carry out vacuum extractions and Caesarean sections.

• There are high standards of hygiene and midwifery.

• Safe blood can be quickly and easily obtained.

• Resuscitation facilities for the newborn are adequate and functioning.

• Neither you nor baby has any significant health problems.

• You have a supportive spouse, partner or relatives.

• Your insurance covers all pregnancy-related conditions, any emergency connected with the birth or post-natal period, and any health problems in the newborn.

Finally, make sure you meet the gynaecologist(s) and the midwives and have a careful look at the health facility before making your choice.

OLDER TRAVELLERS

Age on its own is no barrier to travel, unless it's also associated with ill health. An aunt of the author, 90 this year, still teaches English to groups of children in western China every year for six weeks, at an altitude of 2,500m (8,200ft).

But, of course, you do have to make sure you are fit and well, especially if doing independent travel, going off the beaten track or doing anything especially arduous or exhausting. If you're worried about your health at any age, or you're over 60 or 65, you should plan to have a medical check-up, unless you are going on a simple package holiday.

There's no value in listing any special conditions here: there are too many and the degree to which they may affect you is too varied, though some are mentioned on pages 17–26. You and your doctor should discover them and discuss them together. Do remember, though, about travel health insurance. It's essential. You'll have to shop around for the best deal. Some pre-existing conditions are likely to be excluded, or you'll be charged a higher premium to have them covered.

Before flying, talk to your doctor about how to reduce the risk of getting a DVT (see page 42). During the flight, exercise your lower limbs as much as you can, or massage the calf muscles. Continue any medication you're taking and have it in your hand luggage. Also have a list of medicine names and doses. Have a copy of your recent medical records and a doctor's letter written for any doctor you may need to see in the country you are visiting.

If you have a disability, you and your relatives will need to work out carefully each detail of the trip, especially if you are confined to a wheelchair. Any wheelchair must be robust, lightweight, foldable and as narrow as possible.

Form-filling

Some people may need to complete a MEDIF form, which can be obtained from the International Air Transport Association (IATA) or downloaded from <www.iata.org>. This usually needs to be completed in case of recent severe or significant illness, injury, surgery or hospitalisation, or if you need oxygen or any special equipment on board the flight.

BACK HOME

DO I NEED A MEDICAL CHECK-UP?

See your doctor if you're feeling ill or have serious or persistent symptoms. Get this done at once if you have a fever and you have been in a malarious area.

Some illnesses can be picked up during travel, but do not show up until later. Ones you may want to discuss with your doctor include:

- Dengue fever *(see page 92)*.
- Intestinal parasites *(see page 100)*.
- Bilharzia *(see page 90)*.
- Malaria *(see page 61)*.
- HIV and other STIs *(see page 75)*.
- TB if you have a persistent cough.
- Chagas disease from remote travel in South America.
- Filarial infection from longer-term travel in the tropics.

Doctors disagree about whether Mr/Ms Fit'n'Well need stethoscopes and blood tests when they return from beyond. However, most agree it's worth checking things out with a doctor specialised or experienced in travel or tropical medicine, if any of the following apply to you:

- You've lived in a developing country for six months or more.
- Your style of travel or occupation has put you at special risk.
- You continue to feel unduly tired, stressed or depressed.
- You have recurrent fever or skin rashes that have not cleared, or recurring periods of feeling unwell.
- You've had a bad experience that seems to be affecting your physical or emotional health.

REVERSE CULTURE SHOCK

So you've been abroad for a couple of months, a couple of years? And when you first came back and were met at the airport as the returning hero you felt pretty good? Now for no apparent reason you're feeling listless, anxious and depressed. If you experience these or similar symptoms, don't think the sky is caving in or you're going crazy. By being aware of reverse culture shock before coming back you'll realise the way you may feel is probably nothing to get stressed about.

If you experience reverse culture shock you may become confused about who you are and where you want to be. You may want to hold on to the great experiences and new ideas you had abroad. Often part of you still wants to be abroad, leaving you reluctant to settle back into your own country and its routines. You may feel unsure of your identity, and your old friends may seem to have changed so you no longer feel part of the crowd. Certain people, situations and future events may fill you with dread. You don't want to get back into everything you were into before travelling – materialism, for example.

Friends and family worry about the change in you. After a few carefree days at home you may get moody, become less fun, lose your sense of humour, become very judgemental, bad-tempered, or tearful. All these are part of the normal process.

The Road to Recovery

Things will start looking up as you gradually adapt, catch up on sleep, and meet up with others who've been abroad and who feel much the same as you. You'll begin to see both the good and bad in where you've come from and where you are now.

If the doom and gloom seriously persist, a chat with a friend or counsellor often helps put life back in focus. If you experienced anything particularly stressful on your trip, such as an armed robbery, personal threats, a serious relationship problem, an assignment that failed to work out, or any experience of death, destruction or suffering, counselling may be helpful.

PAUSE FOR THOUGHT

Having dealt with reverse culture shock and sorted out any lingering ailments you may have picked up on your travels, settled back into work or study, or even started to plan your next trip, you'll have a chance to reflect upon the places you've been and the people you've met. Spare a thought for those you've encountered on your travels who may not be as fortunate as yourself. They may not have the same easy access to medical treatment as you do – the World Health Organization's figures show that one-fifth of the world's population has no access to essential health care. If you wish to contribute towards improved health care in developing countries <www.justgiving.com/international-aid-agencies-health> and <www.cfd.wa.gov/charityguide> (US) have links to many major charities.

FURTHER INFORMATION

BOOKS

The Traveller's Good Health Guide, Ted Lankester (Sheldon Press, 2006). More detailed health information in an easy-to-read and logical format.

Your Child Abroad: a Travel Health Guide, J. Wilson-Howarth, M. Ellis (Bradt, 2004). Everything you need to know about travelling with children.

Expedition Medicine, ed. D. Warrell, S. Anderson (Profile Books with Royal Geographical Society, 1998). Full information on expeditions and hostile climates.

Staying Alive, David Lloyd-Roberts (International Committee of the Red Cross, Geneva, 2005). A must-have book if you live in or wander into war zones or unstable areas.

Practical First Aid, British Red Cross (Dorling Kindersley, 2003). Excellent, practical book on handling medical emergencies. Useful for team leaders, health workers and those doing emergency relief and adventure travel.

Travellers' Health, R. Dawood (Oxford University Press, 2002). A comprehensive, 734-page reference book, full of detail.

Setting up Community Health Programmes, Ted Lankester (Macmillan, 2007). Useful if you'll be involved in health work. Available from InterHealth or TALC (email: <info@talcuk.org>).

Urban Health and Development, B. Booth, K. Martin, T. Lankester (Macmillan, 2001). Useful if you'll be doing health or development work in cities or working with street kids.

WEBSITES

Travel Health Suppliers

InterHealth <http://shop.interhealth.org.uk>.

Nomad <www.nomadtravel.co.uk>. Email: <orders@nomadtravel.co.uk>.
Masta <www.masta.org/travel-shop>.
Chinook <www.chinookmed.com> (for US citizens).

Destination-Specific Information

<www.fit-for-travel.scot.nhs.uk>
<www.masta.org>
<www.travelhealth.co.uk>
<www.tripprep.com> (for US citizens)
<www.traveldoctor.com.au> (for Australian citizens)

Official Medical Body Recommendations

World Health Organization <www.who.int/ith>
UK <www.nathnac.org>
UK malaria information <www.malaria-reference.co.uk>
USA <www.cdc.gov/travel/yb>
Worldwide list of doctors and clinics <www.iamat.org>

Other Useful Sites

UK Foreign Office <www.fco.gov.uk/travel/countryadvice>
US Department of State <www.travel.state.gov/travel>
British Mountaineering Council <www.thebmc.co.uk>
Blood Care Foundation <www.bloodcare.org.uk>

SOURCES OF INFORMATION

Information in this book is based on authoritative sources including the World Health Organization, the UK Advisory Committee on Malaria Prevention, the UK National Travel Health Network and Centre (NaTHNaC), Health Protection Scotland, the Centers for Disease Control and Prevention USA, and a number of research papers and reviews in international journals.

INDEX

Berlitz pocket guide

Travel Health

First Edition 2008
Reprinted 2012

Written by Dr Ted Lankester
Edited by John Mapps and Anna Tyler
Series Editor: Tom Stainer

Photography credits
APA/David Abrams 122/Chris Bradley 82/Jon
Davison 40, 74, 123, 124/Glyn Genin 47/David
Henley 53/Britta Jaschinski 59, 61, 119/Shen Kai
12/Bill Wassman 72/Marcus Wilson Smith 21,
48, 97, 101, 110/Gregory Wrona 31, 116; 4
Corners Images 137; Alamy 57, 63, 77, 79, 132;
Alaska Division of Tourism 13, 83; Carnival
Cruises 46; Corbis 6, 18, 50, 90; Getty Images
66; Tony Halliday 55, 85, 114; Adriano
Heitmann; Jim Holmes 94; Kerrick James 39;
David Keith Jones/Images of Africa 106; Link/
Dinodia 121; Mexican Tourist Board 131;
Nature Picture Library 102, 104; Scanpix/
Photolibrary 7; Science Photo Library 37, 64.
Cartoons: © InterHealth
Cover picture: Agence Images/Alamy

All Rights Reserved
© 2008 Berlitz Publishing/Apa
Publications GmbH & Co. Verlag KG,
Singapore Branch, Singapore

Printed in China by CTPS

Berlitz Trademark Reg. U.S. Patent Office
and other countries. Marca Registrada
Used under licence from the Berlitz
Investment Corporation

DISCLAIMER
As far as possible information was correct
at the time of publication. However,
recommendations on travel medicine
frequently change, especially with regard to
immunisation and antimalarial advice. For
this reason, when in doubt check updated
websites listed and consult a travel health
adviser. Although every effort has been
made to ensure accuracy, neither the author
nor the publishers can accept any liability
for unforeseen errors or omissions, or for
any illness or event arising from advice or
information given in this book.

The right of Ted Lankester to be identified
as the Author of the work has been asserted
by him in accordance with the Copyright,
Designs and Patents Act 1988.

No part of this book may be reproduced,
stored in a retrieval system or transmitted in
any form or means electronic, mechanical,
photocopying, recording or otherwise,
without prior written permission from
Berlitz Publishing. Brief text quotations with
use of photographs are exempted for book
review purposes only.

Contact us

At Berlitz we strive to keep our guides as
accurate and up to date as possible, but if you
find anything that has changed then we would
be delighted to hear from you.

Berlitz Publishing, PO Box 7910,
London SE1 1WE, England.
email: berlitz@apaguide.co.uk
www.berlitzpublishing.com